TEACHING UNPREPARED STUDENTS

TEACHING
UNPREPARED
STUDENTS

Strategies for Promoting Success and
Retention in Higher Education

Kathleen F. Gabriel

Foreword by Sandra Flake

STERLING, VIRGINIA

Published by Stylus Publishing, LLC
22883 Quicksilver Drive
Sterling, Virginia 20166-2102

Library of Congress Cataloging-in-Publication Data
Gabriel, Kathleen F. (Kathleen Faye)
    Teaching unprepared students : strategies for promoting
success and retention in higher education / Kathleen F.
Gabriel ; foreword by Sandra Flake.—1st ed.
        p.   cm.
    Includes bibliographical references and index.
    ISBN 978-1-57922-229-1 (cloth : alk. paper)—
    ISBN 978-1-57922-230-7 (pbk. : alk. paper)
    1. Developmental studies programs.   2. Underprepared
college students.   3. College dropouts—Prevention.   I.
Title.
LB2331.2.G33 2008
378.1'25—dc22   2007048785

13-digit ISBN: 978-1-57922-229-1 (cloth)
13-digit ISBN: 978-1-57922-230-7 (paper)

Printed in the United States of America

All first editions printed on acid free paper
that meets the American National Standards Institute
Z39-48 Standard.

Bulk Purchases

Quantity discounts are available for use in workshops
and for staff development.
Call 1-800-232-0223

First Edition, 2008

10   9   8   7

To my husband, Michael, and my children, Stephanie, Isaac, and Lucas. Without their constant support, encouragement, understanding, and love, this book would not have been possible.

CONTENTS

ACKNOWLEDGMENTS   *ix*

FOREWORD   *xi*

1. UNPREPARED AND AT-RISK COLLEGE STUDENTS   *1*
   Myth or Reality?
      Overview
      Conclusion

2. PHILOSOPHICAL FOUNDATIONS   *9*
   Yes, They Can!
      Background
      Lessons From the Best
      Philosophy Crystallized
      Guiding Principles
      Conclusion

3. THE FIRST WEEK OF CLASS   *25*
   Sharing a Mission for Success
      Policy on No-Shows and Late Adds
      Identifying At-Risk Students
      Preplanning: Course Goals and Teaching Philosophy
      Preplanning: Write Intended Learning Outcomes
      Assessment and Grades
      Introduce Learner-Centered Education
      University Resources, Support Centers, and Tips for Success
      Expectations of Behavior
      Syllabus Use and Follow-Up
      Conclusion

4. BEGIN WITH CONSISTENT CONTACT   *41*
   Attendance That Matters
      Benefits of Class Attendance
      Techniques That Increase Class Attendance for At-Risk Students
      Conclusion

5. LEARNING STYLES AND THE SCIENCE OF LEARNING   *57*
   Tapping Brain Power
      Learning Styles and Learning Approaches
      Learning Styles and the Science of Learning

Benefits for Professors
Conclusion

6. EMBRACING LEARNER-CENTERED EDUCATION   *73*
    Engaging Students
    Defining Student Success
    Encouraging and Clarifying Student Responsibility
    Preparing for Resistance
    Establishing a Learning Community
    The Prior Knowledge Factor: Meet Students Where They Are
    Conclusion

7. INTERWEAVING ASSESSMENT AND TEACHING   *87*
    Any Questions?
    Summative and Formative Assessment Differences
    Examples of Formative Assessment Techniques
    Conclusion

8. TECHNIQUES FOR PROMOTING ACADEMIC INTEGRITY
    AND DISCOURAGING CHEATING   *103*
    Playing by the Rules
    Rubrics for Promoting Integrity
    Individual Feedback
    Plagiarism Tutorials
    Universal Design for Instruction
    A Vocabulary Strategy for Improving Comprehension
    Prevention Techniques for Tests
    Know University Standards
    Conclusion

    EPILOGUE: FINAL THOUGHTS   *119*
    Promoting a Richer Campus Environment

    APPENDIX A   Checklist for Possible Course Syllabi Items   *121*
    APPENDIX B   Performance Prognosis Inventory for Analytical Chemistry   *125*
    APPENDIX C   Preparing for Three Different Groupings   *125*
    APPENDIX D   Vocabulary Strategy Steps   *131*

    REFERENCES   *135*

    INDEX   *141*

ACKNOWLEDGMENTS

I am grateful for the support and guidance of several people who generously gave of their time to assist me in writing this book. First, I am deeply indebted to my son, Isaac M. Gabriel, who always made time to discuss, read, and edit all chapters despite his extremely busy schedule. His constant enthusiasm for and interest in this project has been invaluable, and without his help, there would be no book.

I also want to thank and acknowledge the incredible support from several colleagues: Dr. Julia George-Borvay, Ms. Mary Anne Schiavone, Mr. Todd Snedden, Dr. Mary Ellen Pambookian, and Ms. Joanne Walser. Their feedback, meaningful contributions, and edits were significant. In addition, their experience and teaching expertise kept me on the right track.

A very heartfelt thanks to my many students who have given me permission to share their personal stories. Even though most suggested that I use their names, in the end, I changed all of their names in order to respect their privacy.

I am so appreciative of Dr. Sandra Flake for her willingness to review my book and write the foreword. I want to give a very special thank you to John von Knorring, president and publisher of Stylus. I am also grateful to Judy E. Coughlin, production manager at Stylus, for her splendid assistance and careful attention to all the necessary details.

Finally, I am extremely indebted to my husband, "Gabe," for his constant encouragement, unwavering patience, and editorial suggestions. As an outstanding educator for more than 30 years, his instincts and insights were fabulous.

Kathleen F. Gabriel
Chico, California
August 2008

FOREWORD

Kathleen Gabriel's *Teaching Unprepared Students: Strategies for Promoting Success and Retention in Higher Education* is an invaluable tool for college and university faculty whether or not they teach unprepared students. The philosophy underlying the approaches and the strategies Gabriel uses to help students understand how to learn in a college environment are useful for working with all students, including those who are adequately or well prepared to take on college. But, of course, these approaches are best suited and will significantly help students who are challenged by college-level material and who need to develop the skills to succeed in an academic environment.

Earlier in my career I spent several years as a faculty member working with unprepared college students, first in an equal opportunity program at the University of Wisconsin-Milwaukee, and then as director of a reading and writing center and retention programs for students of color and immigrant students at the University of Minnesota's General College. Gabriel's book and her examples immediately brought to mind the impact that teaching students who needed additional preparation for college had on me. I had not realized, until my experience at UW-Milwaukee, that fairly large gaps in skills could be overcome and that students unprepared for college could make large gains if they were challenged and supported in their learning.

The strategies Gabriel outlines work effectively with students who need to develop their skills—particularly once they realize the importance of those skills and how much they will need them. I still remember Vince, who showed no concern about his low grades on two writing assignments but who came into my office greatly concerned when the grade on his third paper indicated only marginal improvement. As he put it, "I knew the first two papers were bad—I rushed them and didn't try. But I knew I could get an A or a B if I tried, and on this one, I tried!" That third paper was the catalyst for Vince; learning how to improve his writing suddenly became important. Vince never became a great writer, but in that semester he took the first major steps to becoming a competent writer. He also learned that to write well, trying was the first step, not the last.

Gabriel recognizes too that students with good abilities may still be unprepared for learning at the college level. Gaps in skills are the result of *not* learning how to study, how to read college-level materials, how to manage time, how to read a syllabus, how to communicate in writing, and so on. Further, students who are ill prepared for higher education often value the credential without valuing the learning that goes along with it.

I highly recommend *Teaching Unprepared Students: Strategies for Promoting Success and Retention in Higher Education* to faculty members who are dedicated to improving student learning. This book promotes improved learning in a context of high expectations. It is a primer for all of us who believe in the value of a rigorous education that fosters development of knowledge and skills for a lifetime. It recognizes that students learn better in an environment where they understand the expectations, where they learn through application and practice, and where multiple pathways to knowledge and skills result in lifelong learning and education. This book also provides useful ideas for those of us engaged in working with a full spectrum of students, from the unprepared and often unengaged to the well-prepared and dedicated learners. Gabriel recognizes there are multiple paths to successful learning, and faculty members can guide students to finding the pathways that help them to be successful.

Let me close with a final recollection. Robin was a factory worker who decided to get an education to improve his standard of living. He came into my office one day near the end of his first semester in college and proudly handed me a book—the first he had ever read without it being required of him. He had come to the university to improve his standard of living and would do so, but he had also improved his understanding of what it meant to be educated. He would now read books on his own, for both learning and enjoyment. Kathleen Gabriel understands that successful students develop the ability to learn enough to get that credential—the degree—and to learn enough to value education beyond the credential. She teaches all of us ways to make that happen.

Sandra M. Flake
Provost and Vice President for Academic Affairs
California State University, Chico

UNPREPARED AND AT-RISK COLLEGE STUDENTS

Myth or Reality?

Not everything that is faced can be changed.
But nothing can be changed until it is faced.

—James Baldwin

The number of academically unprepared and at-risk students enrolling in colleges and universities is increasing. In a national survey of college professors conducted by the *Chronicle of Higher Education*, 44% of college faculty members reported that their students "are ill prepared for the demands of higher education" (Sanoff, 2006, p. 1). Results from the American College Testing Program (ACT) in 2006 support the professors' perception. These results show that 49% of high school graduates do not have the reading skills they need to succeed in college (Kuh, Kinzie, Schuh, Whitt, & Associates, 2005, p. 1). For those who attend college, about 25% of first-time students at 4-year colleges and universities require at least 1 year of remedial courses (Adelman, 2004; Horn & Berger, 2004; Kuh et al., 2005, p. 1).

These statistics may be surprising, but they do not fully describe the attitude of many of today's college students. As Weimer (2002) explains,

> Students now arrive at college less well prepared than they once did. They often lack solid basic skills and now work many hours to pay for college and sometimes a car. . . . Many students lack confidence in themselves as learners and do not make responsible learning decisions. . . . Having little

self-confidence and busy lives motivates many students to look for easy educational options, not ones that push them hard. . . . Obviously, these descriptions are not characteristic of all students, but most faculty quickly agree that teaching college students today is far more challenging than it once was. (pp. 95–96)

For at-risk or unprepared students with inadequate reading and writing skills, college placement tests serve as a barrier to registering for the college English and math classes needed for general education requirements, thus forcing the students to take remedial courses to prepare them for these college-level classes. However, at many institutions, these same students are not prevented from enrolling in social science, humanities, and some science courses, where they can quickly falter. When assessing all students' abilities and attitudes in several specific areas, "faculty members say that students are inadequate writers, have trouble understanding difficult materials, fall short in knowledge of science and math, have poor study habits, and lack motivation" (Sanoff, 2006, p. 1).

While reforms at the high school level have been proposed, many universities and colleges have already established summer programs that target academically at-risk students, first-generation students, and others who traditionally have had low levels of retention and/or college graduation rates. These summer programs seek to set these students on the right path for succeeding in college since "most student attrition occurs during the first year of college" (Wankat, 2002, p. 173). Many colleges have increased their tutoring center services, hired retention specialists, offered developmental courses for unprepared students, and expanded first-year experience programs that target the incoming students.

Still, the statistics of success rates for at-risk students are bleak. Kuh et al. (2005) report "seventy percent of students who took at least one remedial reading course in college do not obtain a degree or certificate within eight years of enrollment" (p. 1). They also report the following:

More than one-fourth of 4-year college students who have to take three or more remedial classes leave college after the first year (Adelman, Community College Survey of Student Engagement (CCSSE) 2005; National

Research Council 2004). In fact, as the number of required developmental courses increases, so do the odds that the student will drop out (Burley, Butner, & Cejda 2001; CCSSE). (Kuh et al. 2005, p. 2)

Many of the at-risk students are doomed to failure either because they are academically disqualified by university officials or because they decide to leave the university with a low grade point average. The cost of losing these students can be high for the students, their families, and the universities that lose them. When universities lose students to academic failure, they not only lose human potential but also real dollars and cents in the form of lost tuition monies, additional resources expended on recruiting replacement students, and so on.

As colleges and universities have examined which students are and are not completing degree programs, the resulting studies reveal that for historically underserved students, graduation rates are significantly lower.

Although greater numbers of minority students are entering college than in previous years, fewer continue to earn degrees compared with non-minorities. Poor college completion rates and the racial-ethnic gap in graduation rates mean that too many students are not acquiring the desired knowledge, skills, and competencies needed for the 21st century. (Kuh, Kinzie, Cruce, Shoup, & Gonyea, 2007, p. 5)

The cost of losing students is worrisome to college officials. In response to the revolving-door scenario, many colleges and universities have added retention coordinators and specialists, and increased academic support beyond the traditional tutoring and writing centers.

Even though the odds are against at-risk and unprepared students, there are those who do make it. Not only have academic support programs improved the chances of success for at-risk students, but so have the actions of individual faculty members. In his study Blose (1999) notes that in selective institutions where faculty and staff have high levels of expectations for all their students, then "regardless of individuals' prior academic history . . . students tend to respond and behave as the faculty expected in a kind of self-fulfilling prophecy" (p. 84). When professors "treated the students as academically capable, and held them to high standards" (p. 84) in an environment of respect, students—all students, even those who were admitted as underachieving or unprepared students—achieve an increased level of performance (p. 84). Thus, low retention and graduation rates for unprepared and at-risk students can be improved, and faculty can have a major impact on accomplishing this.

How professors teach and interact with at-risk students makes the difference. There is a relationship between students' intellectual development and student and faculty interaction (Halawah, 2006). Professors can develop a rapport with their students both in and out of the classroom, and have a "significant positive influence" on students' intellectual and personal development (Halawah, 2006, p. 677). And, as most professors already know, posting office hours and waiting for students to come is not enough. In their study of educationally effective colleges, Kuh et al. (2005) found that "the most successful schools balance academic challenges with various types of support so that students are not left to fend on their own to figure out how to succeed" (p. 181).

As educators, we have an obligation to all of our students, including those who arrive unprepared. As members of an institution and as individual professors, we must use a myriad of actions that will provide unprepared students with real opportunities for success. If we do not, we are simply setting these students up for failure and, at the same time, only pretending we have somehow fulfilled a moral obligation of providing opportunities to our diverse population in today's society. Astin (1999) writes,

> The education of the so-called "remedial" students is the most important educational problem in America today, more important than educational funding, affirmative action, vouchers, merit pay, teacher education, financial aid, curriculum reform and the rest. . . . I would argue that providing effective "remedial" education would do more to alleviate our most serious social and economic problems than almost any other action we could take. (p. 10)

While most institutions have academic support centers that strive to ameliorate the problems of low retention rates of at-risk students, many

professors are looking for answers to address the growing number of unprepared and at-risk students who are enrolled in their courses, who underper-
form, and who are reluctant to seek help. "Much of the existing literature
focuses on developing general theoretical models of help-seeking, but few
offer concrete suggestions for interventions" (Chung & Hsu, 2006, p. 254).
The purpose of this book is to provide professors (and their graduate teaching assistants) with teaching strategies and methods that will promote student engagement and improve performance for all the students in their
classes, but especially for those who are at risk or unprepared, without sacri-
ficing high standards or expectations.

Overview

In chapter 2, "Philosophical Foundations," I explain that articulating a
teaching philosophy can help clarify beliefs and principles about teaching.
After a teaching philosophy is established, it can be used as the guiding
principle for developing teaching goals for each course that we teach. In this
chapter, I describe the five guiding principles that constitute the foundation
of my teaching philosophy, wherein my ultimate goal is to provide opportunities for success for all college students, focusing particularly on giving
unprepared students a real chance to make it.

In chapter 3, "The First Week of Class," I discuss how we can augment
students' enthusiasm and motivation by clearly explaining and identifying
the goals and objectives of the class and the specific procedures and expectations that students must meet to succeed. As professors, we must do this in
the first week of class. Our message should be communicated verbally and
in writing (e.g., the syllabus) so that our students, as well as ourselves, can
refer to the expectations throughout the semester. Chapter 3 addresses the
various components of a learner-centered syllabus and how it can be used as
a guide for student success. If a positive and interactive tone is set during the
first week of the semester, the benefits will be reaped throughout the rest of
the course.

In providing opportunities for interactions with your students and among
your students (i.e., student-to-student contact) is another important ingredient for retention. Chapter 3 also deals with creating an atmosphere for promoting appropriate and engaging behavior and discusses techniques for

creating a positive classroom environment that embraces diversity and promotes inclusion and respect for all. A variety of methods that professors and graduate teaching assistants can use to help students appreciate the benefits of diversity in our society are included.

In chapter 4, "Begin With Consistent Contact," the connection between attendance and retention is examined. Retention begins with a student's success in his or her courses, and achieving success is tied to regular attendance. Several studies show that students who go to class regularly earn higher grades and are more likely to stay in college. This chapter discusses six steps that we as faculty can easily implement that will increase class attendance of all students, regardless of how prepared they may be for college. Furthermore, the ways these steps reinforce Chickering and Gamson's (1987) *Seven Principles for Good Practice in Undergraduate Education* are examined.

Chapter 5, "Learning Styles and the Science of Learning," sets forth several types of learning style inventories students can take that will help shed light on individual learning style preferences. This chapter covers three specific models. Such knowledge can empower students and increase their sense of responsibility in the learning process as they discover new study techniques and methods for different types of learners. In addition I discuss learning approaches and science of learning research. Knowledge of learning styles, learning approaches, and the principles from the science of learning not only helps students but professors also, as we too can evaluate our own teaching styles and make sure that we have a variety of approaches and assessments that play to various student's respective needs.

Chapter 6, "Embracing Learner-Centered Education," familiarizes readers with learner-centered environments. As community colleges and 4-year institutions seek ways to improve their retention and graduation rates, many have recognized that shifting the pedagogy focus from professor centered to learner centered can benefit all students, especially those who are at risk. This chapter defines learner-centered teaching and lists specific steps professors can take to become learner-centered teachers, including establishing course goals, developing desired learning outcomes, creating a learner-centered syllabus, preparing for resistance, and establishing a learning community.

These initial steps will guide professors as they plan lessons and activities that will engage students so that they can fully participate in achieving the desired learning outcomes. This chapter stresses the importance of considering students' prior knowledge or lack of knowledge. "If we ignore or avoid prior knowledge, it will hinder our teaching" (Zull, 2002, p. 108). To help students connect with new material, they must make connections that make sense to them. This chapter not only discusses ways to spark such connections, but it also suggests strategies for helping students find ways to catch up to the new material being presented.

Chapter 7, "Interweaving Assessment and Teaching," describes the benefits of ongoing assessments. As professors, we often ask our students if they have any questions. Usually, the response is silence. Yet, after the first exam is over, professors and students may be disappointed or frustrated with poor results. However, by using different types of assessment techniques and activities before (and in between) exams, professors and students can receive specific feedback on whether students are grasping the material, and on the students' progress in applying, analyzing, synthesizing, or transferring the ideas of the course content. An early warning of problems allows the teacher to intervene quickly to avoid discouraging at-risk students. Chapter 7 also reviews the importance of using different types of activities that not only engage students and increase their participation in class, but also give the professor and students feedback as students prepare to demonstrate what they are learning.

In chapter 8, "Techniques for Promoting Academic Integrity and Discouraging Cheating," I present new ways to combat cheating and improve one's grading systems. During class many professors have encountered the question, "Is it going to be on the test?" While most professors find this question frustrating (or infuriating), it also shows that many students are obsessed with their grades. Because of this obsession, the students appear to be focused on doing well on tests and not necessarily on learning the material. In addition, professors have to contend with cheating on tests and/or students who plagiarize papers. This chapter covers a variety of issues related to grading student performances and, at the same time, provides suggestions for discouraging cheating. By using rubrics, Universal Design strategies, and introducing a vocabulary strategy that can help our students—and particularly those at risk—improve their reading and listening comprehension, we can help students improve the way they prepare for tests, write their papers, and complete other summative assignments. At the same time, we will be promoting student engagement and academic integrity.

Conclusion

I have tried to make this book "professor friendly" for both the veteran and beginner teacher. You can choose the chapters that will best fit your needs, or you can read the book in its entirety. Each chapter offers specific tools and interaction techniques specifically for at-risk or unprepared students relating to the specific subtopic. The table of contents is intended to guide your selections. This book is not a panacea for all problems presented by at-risk and unprepared students, but it is hoped that the concepts and ideas will support your efforts in reaching out to these students. Take the ideas you like, and tweak the ones that don't quite fit your teaching style, but above all, realize that you can make a difference in helping at-risk students learn how to become successful college students.

2

PHILOSOPHICAL
FOUNDATIONS
Yes, They Can!

I have learned that success is to be measured
not so much by the position that one has
reached in life as by the obstacles which he has
overcome while trying to succeed.

—Booker T. Washington

Almost all colleges and universities have mission statements that are "clear and focused" and state "those things that the institution professes to achieve within its unique environment and with the particular resources it has available" (Huba & Freed, 2000, p. 100). Closely related to a college's mission statement is its operating philosophy, which guides the college as it seeks to accomplish its institutional mission. Kuh et al. (2005) define the operating philosophy as follows:

> [It] is composed of tacit understandings about what is important to the institution and its constituents and unspoken but deeply held values and beliefs about students and their education. (p. 27)

Within universities and colleges, various departments often will also devise a mission statement, which fits in with or complements the overall mission of the school. Mission statements and philosophies can set the theme of the school, just as a professor's personal mission statement and teaching philosophy will manifest itself in the professor's teaching style and the way she or he interacts with students.

Some universities specifically include in their mission something about at-risk students. For example, Winston-Salem State University and University of Texas at El Paso "emphasize that every person has the potential to learn [and the institutions are] dedicated to expanding educational opportunity for students who by traditional measures are not expected to succeed in higher education" (Kuh et al., 2005, p. 28). Whether or not a university has included such a declaration as part of its mission statement, many individual faculty members are interested in ensuring opportunities for at-risk students and have included this as part of their personal mission statement and teaching philosophy.

Background

There are college professors who are interested in working with unprepared college students. I know this from personal experience. When I graduated from high school, it looked as though I would not be able to get into the local state college—or survive there even if I did get in. I had low to average high school grades; my initial application to a local college was denied. Following an appeal, I was finally accepted in late July, only one month before school started, under the "special admit" category. I still remember when my freshman-year English professor handed back my first college essay with a large red *F* on the top. To add insult to injury, my professor asked me, in a very sarcastic voice, "How did *you* get into college?"

Fortunately, this experience proved to be an aberration rather than the norm during my college education. Other teachers believed in my ability, and with a lot of hard work and encouragement, I learned how to learn and succeed in college. After college graduation, I was accepted in a teacher-education certification program.

As a high school teacher, I wanted to have an impact on students, especially academically nonproductive or low-performing students. It often happens that some colleagues warn new teachers that older students who have trouble in school are the hardest to reach and that it is probably too late for them to catch up. Primarily because of my own academic experiences, I have always disagreed with this notion, and still do. Even in college I believe it is not too late to learn how to learn. Nevertheless, it takes more than just wishful thinking. As Wyoming Tyus, three-time Olympic Gold Medal winner, put it in a 1988 speech, "You need to have the three *D*s: Drive, Determination, and Desire." College teachers can inspire and support at-risk students, but only if these students reciprocate with their own efforts.

Lessons From the Best

In the past as now, many great teachers connect with students and teach them in a way that no other teacher has throughout those students' lives. These teachers have a unique ability to open the minds of students and allow them to believe that they really can learn and do what so many before have told them they could not do: excel in the classroom. Before my first year of teaching, I decided that I could borrow, learn from, and expand upon the methods and techniques of these special teachers.

One person I learned about was Annie Sullivan, whom I consider to be one of the greatest teachers of all time. Annie Sullivan is known as the miracle worker, and in the film of the same name about her life and work (Penn, Coe, & Gibson, 1962), many of her teaching techniques and beliefs are revealed. To this day, she continues to influence my teaching philosophy by shaping and reinforcing my guiding principles.

The Miracle Worker is about Annie Sullivan's famous pupil Helen Keller, who was deaf and blind. Before Annie arrived, Helen's parents had failed to provide any discipline or structure in their daughter's life, primarily because they felt sorry for her. However, Annie had high expectations for her student because she believed in her ability to learn. She held Helen accountable for her actions, something that no one had ever done. *The Miracle Worker* shows how Annie Sullivan's teaching methods changed her student's life.

One particular scene in *The Miracle Worker* influenced me greatly. At noon at the family dining room table, 8-year-old Helen eats by grabbing food off her parents', brother's, and grandmother's plates. The family ignores her and actually encourages the behavior by moving to the side as she moves around the table. However, when Helen reaches for food on Annie's plate,

Annie blocks her from doing so. The other adults are offended that Annie will not accommodate the "poor child."

Instead Annie asks them to leave, and the first lesson begins. Annie tries to have Helen sit in a chair and eat with a spoon, but Helen fights back. A wrestling match ensues with Annie pulling Helen into a chair and putting a spoon into her hand. Helen resists—she throws the spoon across the room as she kicks, hits, even bites Annie. Annie finds more spoons, and there is more pushing and pulling. The struggle goes on and on.

As the family waits anxiously in the yard, they can hear the commotion from the dining room. Finally, at about four o'clock, it is quiet, and Annie appears with her hair a mess and her glasses bent. She announces to the family that Helen ate from her own plate, with a spoon, and she folded her napkin. Annie said, "The room's a wreck, but her napkin is folded" (Penn et al., 1962).

I realize that working with academically at-risk college students is not the same as working with someone who is physically disabled, like the young Helen Keller. Nonetheless, the general teaching philosophy of accountability, high standards, and expecting appropriate behavior is one that I embrace and have tried to uphold throughout my teaching career. Even when faced with adversity, Annie Sullivan stuck to her principles with true grit and a kind of fortitude all teachers need to have. "Folding a napkin" has become a symbol for me—it represents high expectations and standards, perseverance, and settling for nothing less.

Philosophy Crystallized

While developing a teaching philosophy, we as teachers can learn from watching other professors, as well as by drawing upon our own teaching and learning experiences. Once a philosophy is developed, it can be used as a foundation to guide one's style of teaching and interactions with students. When students fail, or teachers fail to reach them, we should try to figure out why by asking, "What could I have done differently?" When students succeed, we may ask, "What things or conditions helped the students achieve that success?"

I am convinced that no single teacher, class, or support program can be a panacea for all students. Even the programs or colleges that demonstrate high levels of success cannot help every at-risk student. Some professors will inspire some students and will become those students' favorite college professors. The very same professors will have students in their classes who seem impossible to reach. No matter what kind of challenges we have with the different types of students who come to college, we should be consistent with our teaching philosophy. Even if we don't write down a mission statement or teaching philosophy, most of us have basic beliefs about students and teaching that will guide us as we develop policies and practices. Clarifying one's teaching philosophy in writing can be helpful, and it is highly recommended for all teachers. Furthermore, if you have not already done so, consider expanding your teaching philosophy so that it specifically includes at-risk or unprepared students.

Guiding Principles

By purposely considering the unprepared students who traditionally have had low success rates in colleges and universities, we professors can have guiding principles that include all types of students we might have in our courses. The five guiding principles I try to follow as I teach and work with all students—at-risk students in particular—are

1. All students, including those who are unprepared or at risk, can become lifelong learners.
2. Significant change requires commitment and time.
3. Struggle is a necessary and important part of life.
4. Students must accept responsibility for their learning progress.
5. Professors should never do for students what students can do for themselves.

These principles serve as the foundation and core of my teaching philosophy.

Principle One

The belief that at-risk students can become lifelong learners is the key to the other four principles. Even in college it is not too late for students, at-risk or otherwise, to change their academic habits. In fact, it is never too late to discover one's own abilities. Some students are more open to this discovery than others.

If students believe that "one is born with a certain level of ability in an area and it cannot be changed . . . [they] will accept their failure . . . as evidence of the hopelessness of their situation" (Dweck & Leggett, 1988, as cited by Svinicki, 2004, p. 162). However, students who have this frame of mind can be influenced and can change their viewpoints. Svinicki (2004) points out that teachers can change students' beliefs about their ability by modeling and by talking to the students about their efforts. She writes, "If we focus on what can be done and on effort, rather than focusing on some inborn ability, we are both modeling an appropriate belief and encouraging students to reframe their thinking" (p. 162). In addition, by employing learner-centered teaching methods, engaging students, and providing them with corrective feedback on their work, students will be able to chart their own progress and academic improvements.

Once at-risk students discover that they can be successful, they can make tremendous improvements and become excellent (or very good) students. Throughout my teaching career I have had many, many rewarding moments—but the most rewarding ones are when students call or e-mail many years after they have left my class. Seeing students who started college unprepared improve enough to be successful in college, then graduate, continue to grow in their careers, and even go on to graduate school is gratifying. Recently I received a wonderful e-mail from a former student who is now in his thirties and about to go back to graduate school for his master's degree. He wrote, "Can you believe it? Who would have ever thought that I would be doing this—and to beat all, my employer is paying my tuition."

One of the best calls came from a student who was particularly challenging for me when he was a freshman. Now Chancy works with at-risk high school students, just as he once was. He called one day to tell me how "bad" some of the kids behave when he first meets them. As we discussed various teaching methods and activities that he was going to try, I could not resist reminding him that he once was similar to the students he was now helping. Of course he already knew, and we had a good laugh about it.

The unprepared students who were part of the academic support program I directed had very low achievement scores when they started college. None of the students had reading or writing skills that were considered equivalent to the average college freshman's, and some had reading skills as low as the fifth-grade level. In every class I have ever taught in college, there were always some students with academic deficiencies. However, most of these students made significant improvements by the end of the semester.

For those who also participated in the academic support program, improvements were even more dramatic—most improved their reading scores by as much as three to four grade levels during their first year of college. Even though some were still behind, even with this kind of progress, they had made a tremendous leap in a short period of time and were beginning to believe that they could succeed in the college environment. One of the students who saw his scores improve by three grade levels at the end of his first year told me, "I never expected that I could do that! I feel pretty proud." He is simply one example that shows it is never too late to discover one's abilities.

Principle Two

The second guiding principle of my teaching philosophy is the belief that significant change requires commitment and an investment in time from students and professors. It is imperative that students be expected to attend class, pay attention, and participate. Weimer (2002) reminds teachers that even when they invite students to meet with them, some will not come, and professors must understand that we "cannot help students who do not want help" (p. 111). However, those who do take the time to seek advice from their professors and assistance from tutoring centers or other types of academic support programs will often surprise themselves with their academic abilities.

Throughout the years, I have worked with many students who previously had not thrived in the classroom because they lacked the necessary skills. Some students had simply given up on the idea of academic success because of frustration and prior failures. Once these students gave up, they still got through school—not by learning, but by faking it, cheating, and getting friends to help them out. Nearly every one of these students wanted to do well, but after so much failure some had written off all hope. In some cases, if students were cooperative and friendly, instructors or professors simply gave them a passing grade. The smooth path of least resistance had been followed without much participation or effort on their part. Often this made it easier for the adults around these students, but it inhibited the students' ability to develop or progress. For these students to succeed, their commitment to learning and their teachers' willingness to give corresponding support would have to change.

A telling example of the time and effort that students must be willing to devote in order to improve occurred when two freshmen student-athletes, Emma and Mary Anne, were referred to me by their softball coach 6 weeks after the semester had begun. When Emma and Mary Anne came to my office, I had them describe their classes and current grades. Both students had Ds and Fs in every single class, and one of the students began to cry as she gave the details of her grades. As I outlined a semester plan and set up daily times for them to come to my office, both seemed surprised at the frequency of the meetings and a little hesitant to devote so much of their time to "school stuff." Ultimately, however, both agreed to the daily meetings. By the end of the semester, one student had raised all of her grades to Cs, and the other had raised her grades to a B, a C, and three Ds. Instead of potentially flunking out of school or digging themselves into a grade point average deficit that would have been very difficult to overcome to regain their academic eligibility, Emma and Mary Anne were in a good position to build upon their gains, maintain their eligibility, and get on track for graduation. In the spring semester, both earned over a 2.0.

Later both students expressed how grateful they were to have survived that first semester. They also said that they had put in more hours of studying than they ever had—or expected to when we first met. As Emma stated:

> Coach had told us very casually that if we came to see you, you could help us, but we didn't think that meant we had to see you every day. We thought we were going to meet with you a few times, you would give us

some study tips and advice, and that would be it. Then, when you said we would start meeting every week, we thought it would be once or maybe twice a week. We had no idea that it would become part of our daily routine. We were absolutely clueless. And it was an enormous change in time and effort for both of us.

After that first innocuous meeting in my office and after surviving their first semester of college, both students went on to graduate from the university, and one went on to graduate school to earn her teaching certificate.

After being in the education field for many years, it became quite apparent to me that most at-risk students have no idea what it takes to succeed academically at the college level when they first begin. The amount of time and commitment that is demanded from them often comes as a shock. Another freshman student I worked with stated, "I have done more work in four weeks than I did in four years of high school." But he, like others, discovered the benefits of time and dedication.

Students can and will discover their own potential by becoming proactive about their own education. Once involved, they can develop a commitment to the process. Nonetheless, it has to start with students making a commitment to come to class every single day, and to dedicate themselves to put in the substantial time necessary to succeed. At the same time, these students need at least one professor who is willing to spend time guiding them. The extra hours that Emma and Mary Anne put in also meant that I was putting in extra hours. It takes time and commitment to meet with students to guide them on how to get started, to go over course material, to provide corrective feedback on their writings, and so on. Professors who believe in giving at-risk students a chance must make time to work with them, and, of course, at-risk students must also make time to meet with their professors.

Principle Three

The third principle of my teaching philosophy is derived from a very basic observation: struggle is a necessary and important part of life. To illuminate this principle to my students, I have a quotation from Frederick Douglass hanging in my office that reads: "If there is no struggle, there is no progress."

Learning how to work through problems and not give up when things are not going smoothly is vital to success in all aspects of life. There are no quick fixes, and anguish may be involved. Some at-risk students may not want to go through the struggle and exertion that is necessary. Faced with the effort required to achieve academic success, some at-risk students choose to give up, resisting those who are there to help them make changes.

In a college setting, the teaching faculty, retention specialists, and others in various support centers (i.e., multicultural centers, writing labs, tutoring centers, etc.) are well aware of the avoidance behavior of students who miss tutoring appointments and meetings with their professors, and who do not show up for workshops on how to improve one's academic skills (i.e., test taking, note taking, writing, etc.). To counter this type of behavior, Weimer (2002) suggests that professors "need policies and practices that encourage students to encounter themselves as learners, motivate them to become more than what they are, and provide the resources, experiences, and skills they need if they are to move forward in their development" (p. 111).

Fortunately, professors can try a few approaches when attempting to persuade at-risk students to put in the time and effort that is needed to improve. Some reluctant students will be convinced not to miss class when they realize that they will lose eligibility status for extracurricular activities or be in danger of losing their financial aid. Often an academic adviser or counselor can also be helpful. For example, Ruben, an at-risk student who was taking a course I was teaching, asked if I would allow him to drop my class even though the "drop" deadline had passed. I contacted Ruben's academic adviser, and we met with Ruben together. We told him that even though he was failing the class at that time, there was still time to get tutoring, put in extra time, and pass the class. On the other hand, if he dropped the class, he would lose his status as a full-time student because it was too late to add another class. As a part-time student, his financial aid would be jeopardized, and his health insurance might be canceled.

Ruben decided to stick with my class. He started going to tutoring and meeting with me during my office hours every week. Within two weeks, he was improving. He passed my class, and at the end of the semester he told me the following:

Your class—well, really, all my classes were hard. I was flunking everything, but then when the consequences were laid out and at the same time a plan of action was set up to help me, well, it gave me a little glimmer of hope. At first, I didn't think I could do it. But then, after going to tutoring and coming to see you every week, things got better. I couldn't believe how much it helped. I still can't believe that I passed my classes. It was really hard, but I learned a lot.

Another at-risk student, Raymond, shared with me his doubts about his ability to actually succeed in college. After I had worked with him for about 4 months, Raymond came into my office, sat down, and announced, "I can't believe it. I know what's going on in class. I can do this. I'm *not* dumb!" His new perception did not come about easily—he had to exert himself and work hard to get there.

Despite their initial low conception about their chances of success in college, Ruben and Raymond both graduated. It was not easy. At-risk students need to be told from the outset that it will take time, effort, and hard work to be successful.

Principle Four

The fourth principle of my teaching philosophy is that students must accept responsibility for their learning progress. Students, like anyone else, need to have goals and know it is their responsibility to achieve those goals. Believing in a dream can be a big part of accepting responsibility. Dreams do not just happen, and they are not possible without vision and hope.

With patience and tenacity to nurture this hope, we can have a powerful impact on at-risk students. Even though unprepared and at-risk students cannot simply be talked into obtaining self-confidence, the words we use when talking to such students can make a critical difference. Positive and encouraging words can be enriching and inspiring (Urban, 2004). As teachers, we can help facilitate at-risk students' success by inviting them to come see us during office hours to go over the material and/or go to tutoring and support centers. We can also introduce students to learning styles and specific learning strategies that complement their learning style preferences (see chapter 5 for further discussion). However, there is usually an intervening period of time before at-risk students actually gain confidence and understand that they can make it. As students start to accept responsibility for their own progress, their hopes of being able to actually succeed in academics will grow. This never happens quickly, but it can and does happen for many at-risk students, often because a professor or adviser helps them connect with the educational process.

I discovered an extra twist to this particular philosophy when working with students who were also members of an athletic team on a Division 1 college campus. For some, the dream of playing professionally was strong and often competed with the dream of succeeding and graduating from college. Some thought that they had to choose between the two. I never accepted that notion. Student-athletes need to know (or be convinced) that they can strive for both, and that they do not have to sacrifice academic success for athletic success.

We all believe that obtaining an education and participating in the educational system, even with all its flaws, is a key to a fulfilling life. But sometimes we forget that students may not share the vision even though they have enrolled in our institutions. The vision has to be discussed and demonstrated, whether with statistics of graduates' earning power, revealing testimonials of alumni, or connections with the university career placement centers. These kinds of actions may inspire hope for our students but don't absolve students from the need to accept responsibility for their own learning.

Professors can assist students with learning how to be responsible by holding them accountable. I share this part of my philosophy with my students from the first week of class so they all know that no "last-minute deals" or "extra credit" will be offered for making up missed assignments or low test scores. Grading policy and requirements are clearly explained in the syllabus and are also discussed during the first week (see chapters 3 and 6 for further discussion).

Even with reminders, a few students might challenge this policy when they have made poor choices throughout the semester. For example, Claudia, who was an at-risk student with a learning disability, had been pledging a sorority for most of the semester. With every absence or missing assignment, she would give her obligations to the sorority as an excuse. At the end of the semester, she came to my office crying and begging for me not to give her an F, which she had earned. She said, "I'm not asking for you to just give me a higher grade—I will do extra work to earn it." As I handed her a tissue, I reminded her that having a "secret" or "special" deal would not be fair to the rest of the students but, more important, it would not be fair to her. As I handed her more tissue, I told her the following:

> Claudia, you have made choices throughout the semester, and you have chosen not to come see me for help or assistance until now—even though I asked you to in February, in March, and even in April. Now it is May, and it is too late. Next semester, I hope you will make different choices. But, of course, it will be up to you to decide and act on those decisions.

Another student who was failing came to see me before spring break and stated, "I know you are really mad at me." I told him, "I am not mad. I totally respect your decision not to be in my class or in college. However, if that is your decision, drop your classes now before you waste any more money and my time." His jaw dropped. "Well . . . well," he stammered, "I want to be here, and I want to be in your class." I simply replied, "Then show me, John. Show me." He did, and he passed (barely, but he did pass.)

I often post quotations on my office door that epitomize my teaching philosophy. One that relates to this particular principle is from John C. Maxwell's (2007) book *Talent Is Never Enough*. He reminds his readers to "remain teachable" (p. 175). Maxwell adds advice from J. Konrad Hole, who wrote:

> If you cannot be teachable, having talent won't help you.
> If you cannot be flexible, having a goal won't help you.
> If you cannot be grateful, having abundance won't help you.
> If you cannot be mentorable, having a future won't help you.
> If you cannot be durable, having a plan won't help you.
> If you cannot be reachable, having a success won't help you. (as cited in Maxwell, 2007, p. 175)

The advice from Maxwell and Hole reinforces principle four: Students must be responsible for their own learning. As professors, we can help students accept responsibility by holding them accountable.

Principle Five

The final principle of my teaching philosophy is that professors should never do for students what they can do for themselves. In his book, *Wooden: A Lifetime of Observations and Reflections On and Off the Court*, legendary University of California, Los Angeles basketball coach Coach John Wooden (1997) writes, "Why can't we realize that it only weakens those we want to help when we do things for them that they could do for themselves?" (p. 15).

However, there is a caveat with this decree. We should not assume that students know what things or how to do the things they should be doing for themselves. Furthermore, just telling students to do something on their own does not mean they are capable of doing it. We may often have to help at-risk students get started and even teach them how to do what they need to do for themselves so they develop the skills to actually become self-reliant and navigate through the university.

Many at-risk freshmen lack skills such as using the library and finding appropriate sources for research papers. Dominic, an at-risk student in my lower-division class, had trouble recognizing the difference between magazine and journal articles, and he was completely overwhelmed when trying to use the library's online search system. Many freshmen—not just those who are at risk—have the same problem, but Dominic was still confused even after a presentation and demonstration from the university's librarian on how to use the system. When he turned in his assignment, it was completely wrong, with all of his articles drawn not from academic journals but from news magazines.

I asked him for a meeting, and when he arrived at my office, I surprised him with a field trip to the library for a one-on-one session on finding academic journals and learning how to ask the librarian for help. Later he told me, "I had no idea how much I had screwed up the assignment. We never did anything like this at my high school, and we never had any kind of books or magazines in my home. I really thought I had done this assignment right." I asked him why had he not talked to one of the resource librarians for help. He told me, "I was embarrassed to ask them. I guess I didn't really know how or what to ask them. Honestly. I am kind of afraid to even approach those people. . . . I mean, I don't know any of them."

Instead of giving Dominic and others who used incorrect sources an F on the annotated bibliography, I had them redo the bibliographies within a few days. Once they had the proper resources, they were ready to write the assigned paper. But Dominic, and other at-risk students I worked with, discovered more than journal articles. By going to the library and talking to one of the librarians, they were able to learn how to use an extremely valuable and important resource that would be needed throughout their college career.

I also believe that professors should never lower their standards or expectations because they believe such standards or expectations are too high. I often tell my students that I will not lower my standards or expectations because I believe they can achieve what I am asking them to do.

Sometimes a professor or academic adviser compromises with students because the professor (or adviser) does not want them to fail. While we may sometimes be tempted to lower standards to demonstrate a program's success, we also understand that the ultimate test is the students' success. As teachers we must remember that most of the at-risk students have felt smothered in the classroom and overwhelmed in figuring out what to do about it. These students need involvement, not extrication. They should not be rescued or disengaged from their learning problems. They must be the major players in the process. No one can do it for them, but we need to provide the support and opportunity for them to gain the skills.

Conclusion

When working with students, there will be days when everything goes wrong. However, if we know what we believe in and have a sound teaching philosophy and a clear idea of what we want to accomplish, then the principles of our teaching philosophy will see us through the arduous times.

Having a foundation to fall back on can provide teachers with a guide, keep them on course, and help them make decisions that will be consistent with their mission. The five principles described in this chapter not only define my teaching philosophy, but have also bestowed upon me the strength and determination to face many challenges in my profession as a teacher.

3

THE FIRST WEEK OF CLASS
Sharing a Mission for Success

The future does not belong to those who are
content with today. . . . It will belong to those
who can blend passion, reason, and courage in
a personal commitment.

—Robert F. Kennedy

The first week of college may be one of the most important weeks
for us as college professors and for our students because it is during
this time that we set the tone and climate for our courses. During
the first few class meetings—not just the first day—we meet our students,
share with them who we are, present course goals, reveal intended learning
outcomes, spell out class expectations, and set up ground rules. How these
components are introduced to students helps establish the classroom atmosphere that we want to develop, expand, and reinforce throughout the semester. In her book, *Learner-Centered Education*, Weimer (2002) reminds us that

> climates conducive to learning are created by action, not by announce-
> ment. If you want this kind of climate in your classroom, you do not get
> it by including two lines in the syllabus saying that your class will have it.
> It results from actions (and sometimes inaction). You take action to create
> it and, once created, actions necessary to sustain it. (p. 101)

The climate we want to sustain must be introduced from the beginning.
One of the most important actions we take for setting up a positive and

inviting classroom climate that is conducive for learning is to provide a written syllabus. Syllabi should be provided for all students; however, for at-risk
or unprepared students who may not be very good note takers or listeners,
having a well-written syllabus that covers all course procedures, expectations,
reading assignments, grading policies, and so on is crucial. It is the best
preventive measure professors can have in the classroom.

Many professors prepare detailed syllabi before the first day of the semester with all aspects of the course and the course policies spelled out. Other
professors seek input from students before finalizing certain aspects or rules of
the course during the first few class meetings. In the latter case, a supplement
or addendum syllabus should be handed out once the students add their contributions. Course information and policies should always be written down,
so that students can refer to them throughout the semester. Having some kind
of course syllabus is usually required by all colleges and universities and is
considered to be a contract (or formal agreement) between professors and their
students (Baecker, 1998; Parkes & Harris, 2002; Wankat, 2002). Furthermore,
"Your syllabus can be an important point of interaction between you and
your students, both in and out of class" (Grunert, 1997, p. 3).

For at-risk students, a detailed and all-embracing written syllabus (that
is made available as a class handout and not only online) is absolutely essential. Many at-risk students have trouble making inferences about course
requirements and expectations. If these students are the first members of
their family to go to college, calling home for advice is not an option. If they
have a learning disability or are unprepared, they may not be able to ascertain
expectations that are merely implied (or not mentioned at all) in a syllabus.
Asking for clarification can be challenging. If a professor appears cold or
unapproachable in any way, most at-risk students may feel intimidated and
likely will not go to that professor's office for assistance.

When directing an academic support program for at-risk college students, I found that many unprepared students had trouble deciphering their
course syllabi. During the first week of every semester, all the at-risk students
participating in the academic support program brought in their syllabi. I
asked everyone to put exam dates and due dates for major papers or projects
on their semester calendar. As the students began doing this, one student
shouted, "Wow! I have nothing to do in this class until October 3." A few

others responded with similar comments, such as, "Yeah, me too, except I have until October 7."

Before even pointing out the obvious—that there would be readings and class notes to study—I looked over the first student's syllabus and found on the bottom of the last page a statement about pop quizzes on the reading assignments and class participation being part of the final grade. He did not understand that pop quizzes would occur randomly throughout the semester and certainly before the first major exam on October 3. This at-risk student, like many others, had missed very important information about how he would be evaluated. The information was there, but since the syllabus was poorly organized, the at-risk student did not recognize the importance of the scattered information.

As professors, we can reach out to unprepared students by designing syllabi that are welcoming, clear, and thorough. Preplanning and preparation must take place before the syllabus is composed. Also, a syllabus checklist is useful when composing or revising syllabi. Checklists that identify possible subtopics are readily available (see Appendix A for an example of a thorough checklist). The rest of this chapter discusses syllabus components that have specific implications for at-risk students.

Policy on No-Shows and Late Adds

Before the semester begins, as professors, we need to decide what to do about students who are absent for the first or second class meeting, even though they registered for class. At the same time, students who are not registered may request to add the course on the first or second day of class. Before deciding what to do with these students, consider this: During the first class meetings, you will establish the class tone and climate, and if students are not present, they will have missed the activities that create a classroom community. Thus, all students need to be present from the beginning, especially at-risk students. Therefore, I recommend a very strict policy for attendance and dropping or adding courses.

For at-risk and unprepared students, the first week of class is particularly crucial because they begin with a disadvantage in terms of skills and/or academic habits. Students who are not at risk may be able to catch up and connect the dots on their own, but unprepared students who are already academically behind their classmates are even more at risk if they are not in class from the start.

At-risk students must be in class by the second class meeting if the class meets two or three times a week. If it meets only once a week (for 3 or more hours), then by the second class meeting, it is probably too late for them to add the class. In most of my first classes, I will already have gone over the syllabus, conducted ice-breaking activities, and established the course climate. For this reason I do not allow students to add after the first day of class, and I administratively drop any registered student who does not attend the first and second class meetings.

If you are an adjunct faculty member and do not have the minimum number of students on the first day of class needed to sustain the course, I suggest handing out the syllabus and asking students to help recruit more class members. Answer questions before the class is dismissed. Then wait until the next class to see if there are enough students to hold the class. You will be doing at-risk students no favors if you have already started your class and then use them to make up your numbers.

Starting off on the right foot during the first week of class is critical. Most experienced teachers will testify that trying to redirect students later in the semester or undo a climate they are not happy with is very difficult. Professors cannot create a positive class alone. In addition, students need to be involved and to share the responsibility for the class climate, and in order for this to happen they must be present. I have always told my students, "This is our class—not my class." *All* students who are taking the class need to be present from the beginning to make connections with their classmates and with the teacher (see chapter 4 for further discussion).

Identifying At-Risk Students

To reach out to unprepared or at-risk students, it may be helpful to identify who these students are early in the semester. Identifying these students can be difficult; however, student records and informal assignments can reveal unprepared college students. For professors who have access to the campus student information system (SIS), looking at students' SAT or ACT scores can be a clue, but be sure to note whether the test was taken during the students' junior or senior year of high school and if it was taken multiple times. Students who achieved high SAT or ACT scores during their junior year of high school are obviously not at risk, and those with low scores may have improved during their senior year. However, students who take the test multiple times may be at risk. The high school cumulative grade point average and rank can also be helpful. If the student was admitted to the college as a "special admit," it is probably because of his or her poor high school performance.

If you do not have access to SIS information, you can ask your department (or campus) academic advisers or counselors for assistance. Many universities have students sign slips that give counselors and faculty permission to share academic information about them for educational purposes, which protects counselors and faculty from violating any regulations of the Family Educational Rights and Privacy Act of 1974. For older students, SIS will also have their transfer college grades and grades from their current institution.

If you cannot or do not wish to look at students' high school records, you can give your students two simple assignments. First, ask them to write a paragraph on why they are taking your class, on what they hope to learn, and/or on their background knowledge of the topic. When we do this on the first day, it not only gives us insight into our students' writing abilities, but it also serves as a way to get to know a little bit about them. A poorly written sample may be an indicator of a student who is at risk or unprepared for college-level writing.

A second assignment that can be insightful for identifying at-risk students is to have them complete a short reading and then give them questions about the reading. While the writing and reading assignments are not foolproof, at-risk students will probably demonstrate the lowest performance among the class members.

Preplanning: Course Goals and Teaching Philosophy

Whether your class is a new course or one that has been taught for a long time, and whether you are teaching the course for the first time or have taught it for many semesters, I highly recommend completing the Teaching Goals Inventory created by Angelo and Cross (1993) as part of your course preparation and planning.[1] If you are teaching more than one course, you should take the goals inventory for each course. This inventory helps us as professors clarify the focus of the class we are teaching and determine assessable goals. Once specific learning goals are clarified for a particular course, intended learning outcomes can be written. Goals and learning outcomes give professors and students a specific focus and direction for a particular course.

When introducing our goals and intended learning outcomes to our students, it is also a good time to ask them to clarify their own goals for taking the course (Grunert, 1997, p. 3). I pass out 3-x-5-inch cards and ask the students to write down their contact information, tell me why they signed up for the class, and list their personal goals for this particular course. As stated, this in-class activity also helps identify possible at-risk students.

Some professors share their teaching mission and philosophy with their students (see chapter 2 for further discussion). We should never openly identify the at-risk students in our classes, but there are general actions we can take that are beneficial to the entire class and especially advantageous for at-risk students. Giving guidance about our expectations and pointers about how to learn and excel in academics is particularly helpful for at-risk or unprepared students. They also need to hear that help and support is available. Simultaneously, students can be reminded that their success also depends on working hard, using support resources, and putting in a lot of time and effort on their schoolwork. Pascarella and Terenzini (2005) note that "the impact of college is largely determined by individual efforts and involvement in the academic, interpersonal, and extracurricular offerings on a campus . . . [and] students . . . bear major responsibility for any gain they derive from their post secondary experience" (p. 602). All students, especially those at risk, must understand the importance of their own commitment.

---

[1] If you have already done this, it will only take you about 10 minutes to complete it again for any possible revisions you might want to make. The Teaching Goals Inventory is available at http://fm .iowa.uiowa.edu/fmi/xsl/tgi/data_entry.xsl?-db=tgi_data&-lay=Layout01&-view; the hard-copy version is on pp. 20–22 in Angelo and Cross's (1993) *Classroom Assessment Techniques.*

As professors, many of us do not realize the powerful impact we can have on students. Light (2001) found that professors often "dramatically underestimate their influence on students' overall development. According to undergraduates, certain professors exert a profound impact" and made a real difference in their lives (pp. 104–105). In fact, during their senior year when students were asked if they could think of a particular faculty member who had an important impact on them, "89 percent quickly identified a particular professor . . . and got so involved with their explanations that it was hard to shut them off" (p. 104). We, as college professors, can have a positive and lasting influence on at-risk students, and as they struggle to catch up, we can give them confidence and help them become young scholars. By reaching out to connect with at-risk students, we can make a real difference.

One way to reach out is to have individual "office" meetings several times during the semester. Using office hours for required individual meetings to go over assignments or test results, in my experience, is particularly constructive for unprepared students. Most at-risk students respond in a positive way. Kuh, Kinzie, Cruce, Shoup, and Gonyea (2007) recommend "early interventions and sustained attention" for at-risk students (p. 37), and having the individual meetings is one way to support their recommendation.

Preplanning: Write Intended Learning Outcomes

When deciding on learning outcomes for a course, we need to begin by considering our goals for the end of the semester. As professors, we need to ask ourselves the following question: What do I want my students to know, understand, and be able to do with their new knowledge as a result of taking my class? (Huba & Freed, 2000). Huba and Freed also suggest examining "existing course descriptions and syllabi in order to review what is currently being taught" (p. 93) in your department, program, or college for guidance. Furthermore, we should not only tell students what we intend for them to learn, but also why the outcomes are important and how they connect to the college's mission and department goals. This added bit of information is very helpful for unprepared students. Their prior knowledge will be less comprehensive than that of their better-prepared classmates, and when this kind of additional information is given, it can help close the information gap and motivate students.

When writing intended learning outcomes for the end of the semester, we should keep two things in mind. First, learning outcomes should describe what the student will be able to do, not the learning activity that we plan or the teaching activity we are using. Learning outcomes should address the abilities or knowledge our students should be able to demonstrate. Begin learning outcome sentences with the phrase, "[You] should be able to . . ." (Huba & Freed, 2000, p. 99). Second, identify only four to six overall learning outcomes on the course syllabus. They should be general enough to cover the entire course. More specific and detailed learning outcomes can be handed out at the beginning of each individual unit and/or at the beginning of a class meeting (see chapter 6 for further discussion).

Huba and Freed (2000) provide several examples of intended learning outcomes from various disciplines. The following are three examples written for individual courses from three different disciplines:

Environmental Issues: You should be able to "articulate the responsibility of the individual in the sustainable management of energy, soil, water, and plants" (p 109).

Current Issues in U.S. Foreign Policy: You should be able to "make an accurate and engaging oral presentation analyzing one current issue in American foreign policy" (p. 110).

Psychological Measurement: You should be able to "prepare a written summary and interpretation of standardized test results" (p. 110).

All the examples describe what the student will do with the course information, and all of these activities are measurable and can be graded.

Assessment and Grades

Once intended learning outcomes have been identified, we have to determine what kind of acceptable evidence we want to collect from the students.

How do we want our students to demonstrate what they have learned, how will we measure (or assess) their performances, and how will we assign grades? On the syllabus we need to tell students ". . . what they will be held accountable for, what opportunities they will have for practice, and under what conditions they will be assessed" (Stanley & Porter, 2002, p. 12). Planning learning experiences and instruction goes hand in hand when making these decisions. In addition, part of improving the possibility that at-risk students in our courses can achieve the learning outcomes includes how we set up our assessment and grading systems.

Many at-risk students begin the semester with unrealistic goals about the grades they will be able to earn. Then, once the first set of grades is returned (from either first midterms or papers), those at-risk students who earned poor grades will start disengaging as a feeling of despair replaces the previous naive goals. "Students find evaluation the most stressful aspect of college life. . . . We need to reduce the stress, but not eliminate it" (Weimer, 2002, p. 126). To accomplish this, there are several things we can do.

First, we need to have a variety of activities or projects that allow students with different types of learning styles and strengths to demonstrate what they are learning (see chapters 5 and 8 for further discussion). In addition to tests, you can assign, for example, presentations, journals, and research or position papers that can be part of the grading system. Courses that have only one or two midterms and a final only raise the anxiety levels of all students, and "afraid, anxious, and stressed students do not easily focus on learning objectives [or outcomes]" (Weimer, 2002, p. 126).

A second strategy we can employ is to use rubrics for papers, projects, oral presentations, class participation, portfolios, and so on (practically anything to be graded). Rubrics save grading time for professors, provide effective feedback, and promote student learning (Stevens & Levi, 2005). Rubrics are especially helpful for at-risk and unprepared students since the rubric is handed out and discussed in class before students start on the assignment (see chapter 8 for further discussion).

Planning for assessment in between formal (or summative) grades is also important for at-risk students' success (see chapter 7 for further discussion). Many unprepared and at-risk students are insecure about their own academic abilities and need to know that it is okay to ask for help and admit that they don't know how to complete an assignment. As professors, we can let students know that we want them to seek help and talk to us. Finally, when setting up and describing to students how they will be graded, it is important to list the number of points that each project is worth as well as its percentage of the total grade. Clear grading points and percentages are important to allow students to figure out their current grade as the semester progresses (see chapter 8 for further discussion).

Introduce Learner-Centered Education

Grunert (1997) notes that a syllabus will communicate much about the professor's attitude toward students and learning. She writes, "The way in which you communicate your views [in your syllabus] helps students to understand whether your class will be conducted in a formal or informal manner. Communicating an openness to questions, concerns, and dialogue begins with the syllabus" (p. 15). Students need to know when a professor will be using a learner-centered approach, because many of their professors do not use this style.

At first, some students may resist learner-centered teaching methods. Therefore, not only do they need a description of what that means, but they also need to know why we are using active learning methods (Wankat, 2002, p. 48). We can use our syllabus to explain learner-centered education, prepare for resistance, and even illustrate the importance of student engagement through discussion and opening-day class activities. Since learner-centered education is more conducive to various learning styles, many students will recognize the benefits for their own learning right away (see chapters 5 and 6 for further discussion).

University Resources, Support Centers, and Tips for Success

Even though there may be a tutoring center, writing lab, and other support centers on campus, at-risk students need to be informed and reminded during private conversations throughout the semester to use these resources. Just listing these resources on the syllabus is not enough. Professors need to push and use a proactive approach when it comes to unprepared students, because most of them do not realize how far behind they are and what it will take to catch up. Especially for freshmen, there is an unrealistic perception of what they are ready to do. When I asked over 200 at-risk students over a period of 7 years to write down their semester goals, more than 70% wrote that one of their goals was to make straight As. This came from students who were special admits and/or had SAT and ACT scores far below the freshman class average score! When I would question students further about such a goal, a typical response was like the one that I got from Dominic, who told me, "Yeah. I can do this. I am going to work really hard." At the same time, I asked him what exactly did that mean. He said, "You know—I am really going to try hard." I asked, "So can you give me some specifics?" He, like most other at-risk students, could not give me any concrete steps and could not articulate exactly what studying hard meant.

Almost all the at-risk students I worked with had the desire to succeed in college and had high expectations for themselves. They arrived at college with admirable goals. With dedication and the proper support, most would eventually achieve academic success. However, as unprepared freshmen, most were clueless about what exactly they were going to have to do to stay afloat and remain off academic probation during their first year of college.

To help at-risk students realize what they need to do, I have students take a revised version of the Semester Performance Prognosis Inventory, created by Saundra Y. McGuire (personal communication, August 2007), director of the Center for Academic Success, and adjunct professor in the Department of Chemistry at Louisiana State University. McGuire put together a list of various behaviors or study activities that students should consider performing throughout the semester (see Appendix B for the complete inventory). I revised the statements to match the academic strategies that related to the courses I teach. Students are asked to write true or false beside each statement that describes the way they will study for the upcoming semester for a particular class. A few examples from my revised inventory, adapted from McGuire, are as follows:

True or False   I will go to office hours or tutoring regularly to discuss the readings, other assignments, and/or the research paper.

True or False   I will make diagrams and draw pictures of the concepts and vocabulary introduced in class and in the readings.

True or False   I will redo all of the quiz and test items I have missed before the next class session and come to office hours to see if my "corrections" are now correct.

After students mark true or false for each statement, they are asked to add up the number of true marks and then turn the paper over for scoring. On the reverse side, students read the following:

Predicted grades for your performance this semester are provided below:

Number of True Responses	Predicted Grade
12–13	A
9–11	B
6–8	C
3–5	D
2 or less	F

Note that you can change your predicted grade at any point by changing your behavior such that more of the statements are true. (McGuire, 2007)

Strong students may already have most of these behaviors as part of their study habits or study routines, but most at-risk students do not and cannot even come up with such a list. Taking this inventory will give them a list of specific academic behaviors they can choose from. For the at-risk students who do not know how to perform some of the tasks listed, I invite them to come to my office (or the tutoring center) to go over the procedures.

During the first part of the semester, many professors strongly encourage, but do not require, their students to attend tutoring or review sessions. However, once the first exam is graded, it is most likely that some students will have performed poorly. McBrayer (2001) suggests a strategy to help "salvage" these students. For his introductory psychology course, he asked students who earned a test score below 75% to come to his office (within the next 7 days after receiving their test scores) for a private tutorial. They were asked to bring their test, textbook, and class notes for the tutoring session. McBrayer writes that these sessions are well worth the time because he gets to know his students, provide each one with one-on-one instruction, and teach them some study skills. During the session, he not only asks the students to tell him how they prepared for the exam, but also which reading, studying, and test-taking strategies they used. He gives the students feedback on their textbook and lecture notes. At the end of each session, he has students make a revised study plan and set goals for the next test. Finally, the students write down five things they will do differently to help them do better on the next test.

McBrayer (2001) reports that the students who attend the private tutoring session increase their test scores by an average of 10 points, but those who don't attend "showed no consistent signs of improvement on the next exam" (p. 3). McBrayer has used this tutoring system for over 8 years and collected data on 547 students, and while he does not indicate if the students who performed poorly were identified as unprepared or at risk, these students are identified as the ones in his class who initially had the poorest performance.

The inventory and the private tutoring sessions are just two examples of actions that we as professors can take in addition to informing students about support centers on campus.

Expectations of Behavior

Somewhere on the syllabus, we can reach out to at-risk students by telling them that we *expect* anyone with a disability (learning or otherwise) to bring his or her letter of identification from the university's disabled student services office. At the same time, we can ask students who are unsure of their college preparation or readiness for college to come to our office to discuss study techniques for being successful in class. We also need to make it clear that in no way does this mean that any standards or expectations will be lowered, but that we are talking about sharing strategies with students for being successful in class. On the first day, I also tell them that I *expect* everyone to attend every class (see chapter 4 for further discussion).

For this part of the syllabus, a statement about academic integrity is usually included along with any test-taking procedures, due dates, makeup policies, and so on. Chapter 8 is devoted to this subject and includes several suggestions for syllabus statements depending on the college, department, and/or the professor's policies.

In addition, statements regarding classroom decorum, etiquette, and ground rules are also included on a thorough syllabus (see chapter 4 for further discussion). It is important to create a climate where students are respectful to each other and to you.

Whatever expectations we have for our students, and whether an individual professor wishes to spell out expectations on a syllabus before the first day of class or whether a professor likes to have his or her students participate in determining those expectations, they do need to be written down on the syllabus. "A thorough syllabus reduces the number of student questions and challenges to course policies during the term" (Wankat, 2002, p. 48).

Syllabus Use and Follow-Up

The learner-centered syllabus can be used as a guide for student success. Parkes and Harris (2002) recommend using your syllabus as a learning tool. All students benefit from a detailed syllabus that will "tell [them] where they will end up when the semester is over and how they will get there" (Wankat, 2002, p. 48). However, at-risk students also need guidance on how to read and use it.

Many professors who go over the class syllabus in great detail on the first day of class will still have students who will miss important management information or other course logistics. To avoid this inevitable situation, Raymark and Connor-Green (2002) recommend giving a quiz on the syllabus that is structured in such a way that students assume the role of the instructor to answer the questions. Raymark and Connor-Green asked questions like "Rebecca asks whether it is possible to meet with you outside of regularly scheduled office hours"; "Veronica has an A average going into the final exam. Now she wants to know why she can't be exempt from the final exam"; "Ann asks you to explain the purpose of the research participation points" (p. 287). Raymark and Connor-Green framed the questions in this way to get the students to consider not just what the course policies are but also the reasons for course policies. They also suggest that the syllabus quiz be required and not offered as an extra-credit option.

I have used the syllabus quiz with much success. First, I have students take the quiz alone. Next, I have them separate into small groups (no more than three people to a group) to compare answers. Finally, we have a total class discussion on any remaining questions students may have about their answers. This approach is beneficial for at-risk students even if they have a low score on their individual test, because they learn the information in a small-group setting.

If we want students to read and use the syllabus, then as professors we must turn to our syllabus often and "encourage students to develop the habit of using it as a common reference throughout the course" (Grunert, 1997, p. 20). When introducing new units of study or new assignments always refer students to your syllabus. After the initial introduction, if we use the syllabus and refer to it throughout the semester, it will be the useful communication tool you intended it to be.

Conclusion

As professors we can use our syllabi as the first line of communication with our students. Also we can (and should) convey our enthusiasm for teaching in our syllabi, the goals and intended learning outcomes that we have for the students taking the class, as well as the teaching mission. Once the syllabus is ready for the first day, it can be used to help create a positive classroom atmosphere.

The syllabus will be the contract between ourselves and our students; therefore, throughout the semester, it will provide direction and focus for our course. For best results, all aspects of the course should be spelled out so the students are on board with the mission of the class, ground rules, expectations for classroom manners, and so on. Having a clear, well-written syllabus can help guide the way for at-risk students as they learn how to be academically successful.

4

BEGIN WITH
CONSISTENT CONTACT
Attendance That Matters

Every noble work is at first impossible.

—Thomas Carlyle

While there may be many factors that influence students' achievement and success in college, students' performance in individual courses may be one of the most determinative. Even if all else goes well, students who fail too many classes or perform poorly are academically dismissed. In response to the importance of students' success rates in individual courses, some colleges target specific courses with additional support, such as adding tutoring, preceptors, and/or supplemental instruction to boost performance. Regardless of whether extra support exists, professors can analyze and improve their teaching techniques to positively influence student performance—particularly for at-risk students. Specifically, all instructors can use techniques to promote student attendance, which in turn can produce higher student achievement and success.

Benefits of Class Attendance

Students who go to class regularly not only earn higher grades, but they are also more likely to stay enrolled in school (Brocato, 1989; Friedman, Rodriguez, & McComb, 2001; McCutcheon, 1989; Sleigh, Ritzer, & Casey, 2002). In contrast, when students' attendance becomes inconsistent, they are less engaged, even when they do come to class. Several studies on class atten-dance found that "excessive absenteeism may lead to the feeling that one's academic situation is a lost cause, and ultimately to dropping out [of school]" (McCutcheon, 1989, p. 1). If students with high absenteeism do not drop out, educators know from personal experience and research studies that these students have lower grades (Brocato, 1989; McCutcheon, 1989). When surveyed, both students and faculty agree that the final grade depends greatly on attendance (Sleigh et al., 2002, p. 54). Thus, when seeking to improve retention and student success, improving the students' attendance for indi-vidual courses is a key ingredient.

At college orientations, deans and academic counselors often talk to new students about the importance of going to every class session, arriving on time, and staying for the entire period. Although they are advised about the benefits of class attendance and warned about the dangers of absenteeism, students may still miss class. Throughout the semester, professors with a class that meets two or three times a week know that all their students are likely to miss at least one or two classes by the end of the semester, and some will even miss three classes. A few absences are usually considered acceptable and not damaging to a student's final grade, but several absences (e.g., more than three or four) are not.

Perfect attendance appears to be a rare thing, yet students who begin the semester with consistent class attendance have a greater chance of becoming engaged in the class and sticking with it, despite its scholarly difficulty. Con-versely, students who begin the semester with inconsistent attendance are less likely to connect with the course and persist. Thus, finding ways to increase class attendance from the get-go will not only help students earn higher grades, but also help students increase their commitment to persevere in college.

Techniques That Increase Class Attendance for At-Risk Students

Methods typically used by faculty with academically prepared students may not be compelling enough (or obvious enough) to positively affect at-risk or unprepared students. Simply saying, "Don't miss class" or "If you attend, you will do better in my class" may get the message across to students who already have a propensity for attending class, but it won't to those who are most likely to miss class. Furthermore, simply including a nebulous statement about a small amount of points for "class participation" as part of the final grade often does not make much of a difference for at-risk students.

So what are we to do? Fortunately, we as faculty can easily implement six steps that will increase class attendance of *all* students, regardless of how prepared they may be for college:

1. Learn the students' names.
2. Help students learn their classmates' names.
3. Require a respectful classroom atmosphere.
4. Demonstrate a positive attitude toward the students and enthusiasm for the subject matter.
5. Use interactive lecture methods with meaningful in-class activities.
6. Take roll and redefine class participation points.

A detailed discussion of the steps follows.

Learn the Students' Names

Professors who learn their students' names not only have better attendance in their classes, but also a better rapport with their students (Wankat, 2002, p. 125). Students respond positively when an instructor recognizes them by name and calls on them using their name. When professors do not know their students' names, students may feel they are anonymous. While most of us may agree that learning students' names is a worthwhile and important task, doing so, especially with large classes, may seem impossible. However, many professors have found ways to accomplish this task. For larger classes, some professors take pictures of the students during the first week of class, label the pictures, and place them in alphabetical order (or use a seating chart) so that they can review students' names and/or faces. Wankat (2002) suggests that instructors bring the photos to class and study them while students are taking a test (p. 126).

Another way to learn names is to make nameplates for all your students. Any office supply store has blank forms, or you can make "tents" from regular letter-size paper. Have students write their names on their nameplates with a marker in large letters, or type in the students' names yourself using a large font size. Then, students can pick up their nameplates as they enter the room and place them on their desks. Not only does this help you to learn their names, but it also helps students learn each other's names. I have found that most students do not like wearing name tags, but they seem to really appreciate having nameplates.

Wankat (2002) also describes informal methods that professors can use when the class size is modest (less than 40 students):

> Come early and look over the class list as students enter. Ask students who they are and if necessary, how to pronounce their names. Write down the pronunciation phonetically on the class list if this will help you remember. Practice using their names. If a student comes to your office hours and you can't remember his/her name, ask. Students appreciate a professor's effort to learn their names and do not mind the professor's asking. (p. 125)

For smaller classes (less than 20 students), I also have used a name game where students stand or sit in a circle. To begin, the first student says his or her name and his or her favorite toy or candy as a child. Then, the next person does the same and repeats what the first person said. This process continues, and as we go around the room, each student first introduces himself or herself and then repeats the name and favorite toy (or candy) for each person who has gone before. It has always been a fun activity, and students always seem to have a good time with it. (For those students who think they have a bad memory, we give hints to help them out.) Students often laugh and enjoy themselves throughout the exercise. You can develop your own variations that will fit your course situation.

There are two additional techniques that I recommend for learning names, which take more time but can have a very positive impact on student attendance. One is to offer some number of points for all students who come to office hours for an interview at the beginning of the semester (or you can require students to come). Extra office hours are added during the first several weeks of the semester so there are plenty of appointment times available for the students. During the short (10- to 15-minute) interview, ask the students questions about where they grew up; why they chose the university; and, in particular, why they are taking your class. This simple assignment reinforces one of the "Seven Principles for Good Practice in Undergraduate Education" (Chickering & Gamson, 1987), which is to encourage contact between students and faculty:

> Frequent student-faculty contact in and out of classes is the most important factor in student motivation and involvement. Faculty concern helps students get through rough times and keep on working. Knowing a few faculty members well enhances students' intellectual commitment and encourages them to think about their own values and future plans. (p. 3)

The initial requirement of having to come to a professor's office for an introductory chat will help ease the way in the future for those students who are hesitant or nervous about talking to professors. If you adopt this technique, it is important to remind the students during class hours if they still need to make an appointment. This kind of follow-through demonstrates your commitment to meeting your students. In addition, this kind of feedback motivates students to do what has been asked of them.

An outstanding professor I met at the University of Arizona has found an innovative way to learn the names of his students, even with his large classes of more than 100 students. On the first day of class, he brings a videotape recorder, and as students are filling out information sheets and reading through the syllabus, he calls them up one at a time for a brief 1- to 2-minute interview that he records. He told me, "The first thing I have the students do is to say their names, because they rarely mispronounce their own names!" All the students have a chance to say a few things about themselves. Then this professor takes the tape home and memorizes all the students' names. At the next class meeting, he stands at the door and greets students by name as they enter the classroom. Needless to say, his students are quite impressed and rarely miss class meetings.

Help Students Learn Their Classmates' Names

A second principle of good practice in undergraduate education (Chickering & Gamson, 1987) is to develop "reciprocity and cooperation among students" (p. 1). When students are introduced to each other and know their classmates' names, it can be the beginning of building a classroom community. With a classroom community atmosphere, attendance rises. It is comforting and inviting for students to go to a class where they know other people, and they are able to talk to each other about the course material or just casually.

By setting aside a little classroom time so that students can meet each other, professors can start the cooperation process. Then when it comes to in-class activities, whether a class discussion or a group project, students who know each other by name will find it easier to work together. Additionally, students will find it easier to create study groups or find a study partner between class meetings. Light (2001) found that "almost all students who are struggling academically . . . always study alone" (p. 40). Suggesting to these students that they should study with others is a fairly simple thing for faculty members or advisers to do. However, finding someone to study with is not always easy for at-risk students. Rather than just tell students to do this, professors can assist in this process by setting up a way for students to meet each other in class and learn each other's names. When this happens in class, it is easier for all students to find a study group or partner, but especially for at-risk students. Light (2001) also suggests that professors consider creating study groups if their students do not do so on their own, as "many students report that working in small groups enhances their engagement with course material" (p. 53).

There are many types of ice-breaker activities that stimulate interaction among students and present an opportunity for students to meet each other. The following are three of my favorites:

1. "Find Someone Who . . ." is one activity that is easy to prepare for and takes only about 5 to 10 minutes of class time. To prepare, create a handout (see Figure 4.1) with instructions and a list of statements (at least 8 to 10) that have to do with the class and/or outside activities. Students then move around the room talking to each other and asking which of the statements they agree with and asking students to sign their name under the statement that is true for them.

FIGURE 4.1
Sample Handout for Activity for Students to Meet Each Other

Find Someone Who . . .

INSTRUCTIONS: BELOW ARE SOME STATEMENTS, AND YOUR TASK IS TO FIND A PERSON IN THIS CLASS WHO AGREES WITH THE STATEMENT AND OBTAIN HIS OR HER SIGNATURE. (NOTE—EACH CLASSMATE CAN ONLY SIGN FOR ONE STATEMENT.) YOU HAVE 5 MINUTES TO SEE HOW MANY SIGNATURES YOU CAN OBTAIN.

Find someone who

    1) Likes to golf

    2) Is from your hometown (or state)

    3) Is majoring (or thinking about it) in geography

    4) Has traveled to Europe, etc.

2. A second ice-breaker activity involves students in making a "Coat of Arms" with a partner's help (F. Sopper, personal communication July 31, 2001). This activity is appropriate for smaller classes. Each student is given a large piece of poster paper and a few color markers. In the front of the room, an illustration of a coat of arms is displayed (see Figures 4.2 and 4.3).

   All the students work with a partner, even though everyone makes his or her own coat of arms. Once finished, students tape their posters up on the wall. Then students take turns introducing their partner and explaining their partner's coat of arms. Even the shyest students seem to be at ease when introducing someone else. The structure of the coat of arms icebreaker keeps the introductions short and interesting.

3. My third icebreaker is called "Thirty-Second Introductions" (modified from an activity described by Murphy [2005]), which can be used with very large classes (more than 100). To begin, directions

FIGURE 4.2
Coat of Arms Directions Example

Draw a symbol that represents you (or your interest/hobby)	Write a motto for yourself
Your hometown or where you call home	Major you are interested in

FIGURE 4.3
Sample of PowerPoint Slide for the Coat of Arms Activity

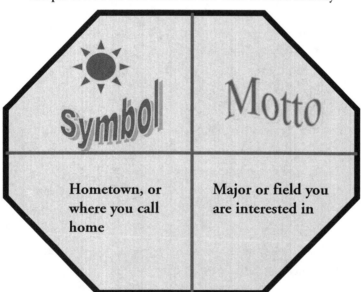

with topics listed (see Figure 4.4) are shown on a PowerPoint slide so everyone can easily see them (Ledlow, 2005). Explain to the class that they will have a chance to visit with several classmates to share their responses to the topic statements. However, the visit, or exchange of information, will be for only 30 seconds. Once they begin, blow a whistle every 30 seconds, and when the students hear the whistle, they are to stop talking to whomever they are with and go talk to someone else. After being sure that everyone understands the directions, blow the whistle to begin.

As students talk to each other, they introduce themselves to another student, following the directions in Figure 4.4. First, each student states his or her name and two of the things listed in the first box. Then, the student can answer one (and only one) of the choices listed in the second box. Every 30 seconds, at the sound of the whistle, everyone moves and finds a new person to talk to. For the next 3, 4, or even 5 minutes, people are visiting

FIGURE 4.4
Questions for the Thirty-Second Introductions Activity

1) **Name, plus *two* of these:**
   - High School Alma Mater
   - Pets, Kids, Both, Neither
   - Home State
   - First, Middle, Last, Only Child

2) **And *one* of these (*in one sentence*):**
   - Possible career for major you are considering
   - Your favorite class (or teacher) in elementary, middle, or high school
   - What you're doing (or wish you could be doing) when you are not at school or working
   - Something about you few people know

with each other, then moving to a new person to talk to every 30 seconds. To conclude the exercise, the instructor announces to the students that it is time to return to their seats. This activity allows students to meet several other students in the class, most of whom they have never met before. It is fast, enjoyable, and serves the purpose of breaking the ice, which will provide a foundation for student interaction.

Many other types of activities can be used to have students meet each other. The purpose of these activities is to encourage peers to interact. Building on the ice-breaker activities, the instructor must commit to continuing to have students interact with each other "in educationally purposeful ways" (Kuh et al., 2005, p. 248). Effective faculty members "recognize the value of peer interaction and facilitate such contracts by designing group projects that bring students together to work on intellectual tasks" (p. 249). For at-risk students, this kind of interaction is vital.

Require a Respectful Classroom Atmosphere

Ground rules on respect must be stated on the first day of class, and a statement describing such expectations should be in the course syllabus. Some professors write a simple statement, such as, "All students are expected to be reasonable and respectful to fellow students, guest speakers, and me." In classes where topics are controversial and stir up a lot of emotion, some professors use more explicit descriptions of what is expected. The following is an excellent example:

> This class is to be a "judgment-free zone" at all times. This means that even if you disagree with somebody's opinion about a subject, you do not have the right to sling any sort of insult, raise your voice, or criticize. I do encourage disagreement, and discussions often are livelier if people have dissenting views about a subject. However, civil/polite disagreement and hostility are two different things. I will not tolerate hostility in the classroom, and will ask anyone participating in this behavior to leave for the remainder of the class period. (Auf der Heide, personal communication, 2005)

Once the expectation for respect is clearly stated, you, as the professor and leader of the class, must not ignore any inappropriate behavior. Hostile issues or rude behavior between or among students should be addressed immediately (see chapter 6 for further discussion).

Demonstrate a Positive Attitude Toward the Students and Enthusiasm for the Subject Matter

When professors have a positive attitude toward students, it not only influences the students' attendance, but also the students' motivation in the class (Jaasma & Koper, 1999; Sleigh et al., 2002). A positive attitude can be demonstrated in several ways, including arriving early to class, smiling and saying hello to students as they enter, asking about their weekend, asking if they had any questions about the reading, and so on (of course, as we've already seen, learning students' names makes a good start at demonstrating a positive attitude toward students). Being available before and after class and having office hours are excellent ways to build rapport with the students. As Wankat (2002) points outs, "Students interpret availability as a sign that the professor cares. . . . Invite specific students to come and talk to you. . . . List your office hours in the syllabus and post them on your office door. Make it clear that you are also available by appointment" (p. 131).

For many students, especially at-risk students, visiting a professor at his or her office is very intimidating, and they are nervous about going. However, if you have been approachable in class, this can help students summon up the courage to come to the office. Besides encouraging students to take advantage of office hours, you can require students to pick up their papers or tests at your office. If students have to come for these items, it provides an opportunity for informal interaction and for giving individual feedback and encouragement.

Some instructors and professors use e-mail as a way to communicate with students. While e-mail may be convenient, it is important to remember that e-mails can have drawbacks, as they can be interpreted as impersonal. As stated by Kussmaul, Dunn, Bagley, and Watnik, "It is easier to misinterpret e-mail than face-to-face communication . . . and some students do not have easy access to e-mail" (as cited in Wankat, 2002, p. 132). Thus, e-mail should never be the only way to communicate with students or be used to replace all face-to-face meetings. It is important to make time outside class for students. Kuh et al. (2005) found that at colleges and universities with the strongest performances in promoting student success, "faculty and staff members make a lot of time for students. They recognize that there is no substitution for human contact, whether face-to-face or via e-mail" (p. 88). Reaching out and showing an interest in students, especially at-risk students, can make a difference in students' attendance habits and in their success rates.

In addition to demonstrating a positive attitude toward students, faculty should also exhibit their enthusiasm for their subject matter. A professor, Dr. Nona Tollefson, who taught a required statistics course at the University of Kansas offers an excellent example (Dr. Nona Tollefson, personal communication, August 30 1988). Tollefson knew that most of her students were dreading the class, and on the very first day she was determined to dispel the negative attitude. She began with a big smile and lots of energy by announcing, "You are going to love this class! It is going to be great." She went on to give the class specific examples of how useful the knowledge they gained would be in other areas of the students' studies and careers. She concluded, "I love teaching statistics because it is one of the most useful tools you will learn to use all through college and indeed all through life. We are going to have such a great time in here! And we will begin right now." Professor Tollefson then had the students complete a simple exercise relating to statistics. Within 10 minutes everyone in the class was comparing answers and discussing the results. At the end of the hour, Tollefson wrapped up by saying, "You know, in most classes, on the first day not much is done except to cover the syllabus—but here, you have gotten your money's worth. You are paying for your college education. So every day that we meet, we will make the most of our class time. By the end of the semester, you are going to love statistics as much as I do! I just know it."

The entire class walked out of the room with big smiles. Tollefson's enthusiasm was contagious, and it had rubbed off on the students.

We don't all have the oomph to do what Tollefson did, and her approach may not be in character for some of us, but if we love our subject matter and can find an appropriate way to share our excitement with students, it will have a positive effect. Most students will respond by making extra efforts to be in class.

Use Interactive Lecture Methods With Meaningful In-Class Activities

Engaging students in a variety of meaningful educational tasks during the class period can dramatically affect student performance and enthusiasm for the class and the subject matter. Simply sitting and listening to lectures is not only boring, but more notably, research studies reveal that most students do not listen for the entire class time, and "fifty minutes of straight lecturing does not work" (Wankat, 2002, p. 68). Students who feel lost in class and are unable to take notes often seek other ways to get the material without having to be in class. For example, being able to get notes that are posted on the Web, or better yet, simply downloading the lecture on an iPod provides students with additional justifications for not coming to class. Furthermore, students are more likely to be absent from classes where they find the teacher boring (Van Blerkom, 1992; Wyatt, 1992).

The solution lies in changing what goes on during the 50 to 75 minutes of scheduled class time. Instead of the typical lecture for the entire period (where a student's role is to sit, listen, and take notes), we need to use meaningful educational tasks to allow students to write, share, report, or solve problems. These kinds of structured activities will increase class attendance and encourage active learning, which is another principle of good practice. As Chickering and Gamson (1987) point out, "Learning is not a spectator sport. Students do not learn much just by sitting in classes and listening to teachers. . . . They must talk about what they are learning, write about it, relate it to past experiences and apply it to their daily lives" (p. 4). There are a myriad of activities and tasks to choose from and many examples are described and discussed in this book. When professors create meaningful educational tasks, most students will find class time worthwhile, have fewer absences, and learn more.

Take Roll and Redefine Class Participation Points

Friedman et al. (2001) found that when there was an attendance-taking policy, and students' absences affected their final grade, attendance was increased (p. 129). One popular way of keeping track of attendance is for the instructor to pass around a piece of paper for students to sign their names on. This sign-in-on-a-piece-of-paper method is ineffective and inefficient. To begin with, it is very impersonal and makes students feel like numbers, especially when the teacher makes no attempt to connect a signature to the real live person who is actually signing the paper. To make matters worse, often it is a graduate assistant who reviews the list of signed names and marks the attendance record. The teacher's concern for attendance appears to many students to be superficial.

Another problem with the sign-in sheet is that it is often circulated during most of the class period. Thus, being on time or staying the entire class period becomes irrelevant. On numerous occasions at the end of the class, I have observed an instructor announce, "Make sure you have signed the attendance sheet." At this point, students who arrived for the last 10 minutes of class race up to the teacher's podium to add their names. Some students sign in and leave soon after the class begins. The message to the student is clear: show up for less then 10% of the class and still get full attendance (or participation) points as long as the student signs his or her name on the paper.

Sign-in sheets can also lead to other problems such as cheating or plagiarism. A student may be tempted to have a classmate sign in for him or her because it requires no interaction between the professor and the student. Using sign-in sheets for calculating participation points reduces the student to just a body in the seat. By creating such initial low expectations, faculty will often get what they have asked for—instead of actively engaged students, they get students who are sleeping, reading newspapers, or text messaging on their cell phone.

There are other efficient ways to take roll that do not include passing around a sign-in sheet or reading a roll sheet and having students respond verbally. Nameplates (discussed on pp. 43–44) constitute one example for taking roll and learning the students' names. Alternatively, you could arrive early and mark students present on the roll sheet as they enter the room and take their seats. Since most students will sit in the same seat (even without a seating chart), it might be easier just to make a note of any students not present as class begins. However, this is not always possible.

Therefore, I recommend redefining and renaming what are often referred to as "participation points" on the course syllabus.

In the course syllabus, "Class Activity Points" should be clearly defined and explained as part of the way that students will be evaluated. Students need to know that simply sitting in class will not get anyone points, and if students are absent, they will not have an opportunity to earn class activity points. In the following example of a course syllabus statement, students are given a clear explanation of how their class attendance will affect their course grade:

> *Class Activity Points* are earned during class time. At every class meeting, we will have meaningful educational activities that will help you grasp the course content; therefore, it is important to make every effort *not* to be absent. Please note that *Class Activity Points* cannot be made up. Thus, if you have to be absent more than twice, your final grade will be affected. Furthermore, I expect you to come to class prepared with all reading and other assignments completed. Just being in class does not guarantee you any *Class Activity Points*. I expect everyone to contribute to and participate in all class activities.

I believe that what ultimately drives the attendance record comes from having class activity points as part of the course grade. The point of all the class activities is not just to take roll. They give students the opportunity to do several things that Kuh et al. (2005) state are essential ingredients for student success: "to practice what they are learning in the classroom, develop leadership skills, and work with people from different backgrounds" (p. 69).

When class activity points are included as part of the students' grade, it will make it obvious to the students (some of whom would otherwise miss the point) that their presence and participation in class is an important part of their college education. Of course, professors will require students to study, read, and complete projects outside class. Still, by providing meaningful educational activities in class, whether it is for several minutes at the beginning, middle, and end of class or for the entire class period, class attendance becomes all the more essential.

Conclusion

The six methods described in this chapter are positive approaches we professors can use to increase class attendance. These techniques also demonstrate to the students that we value them individually and look forward to interacting with and learning from them in class. Of course, when we have classes that have fewer than 50 students, it is easier to implement the methods in this chapter. Large colleges and universities with high levels of student engagement and high graduation rates have been able to provide their students with smaller classes by trying various approaches, "including reducing the size of some classes by increasing the size of others, thus increasing the odds that at least one course a semester would be small enough so that students could actively participate" (Kuh et al., 2005, p. 303). Still, whether you are at a 4-year university or a 2-year community college, keeping the class size smaller can be helpful in promoting class attendance. Even if you have larger classes, the methods described in this chapter can be modified and used with the help of graduate teaching assistants.

Several of these methods also reinforce the concept of valuing student interaction. The methods presented are solidly researched and have been used with much success by many professors. They can create a climate for encouraging students to be enthusiastic and upbeat, willing to come to class, and ready to enjoy the learning experience.

5

LEARNING STYLES AND THE SCIENCE OF LEARNING

Tapping Brain Power

The greatest discovery of my generation is that
a human being can alter his life by altering his
attitudes of mind.

—William James

W hen discussing postsecondary students and factors that promote their success, learning styles are usually included in the conversation. Specifically, it is often recommended that teachers use instructional approaches that are aligned or complement students' preferred learning styles (Bourner, 1997; Kuh, Kinzie, Buckley, Bridges, & Hayek, 2006; McKeachie, 2002). Accommodating the different learning styles of students in one's classroom can at first appear to be a daunting task, especially if we and our students do not know everyone's learning style preferences. In addition to our teaching approaches, many students ask for help on how to prepare for exams. Not knowing individual learning styles makes it difficult to give appropriate advice.

As faculty who are experts in our fields of study and take our tacit knowledge for granted, we may fail to give students specific information on how to use learning strategies that will help them master the material in a meaningful way. While we need not be experts on the different kinds of approaches students might use for studying effectively to understand and to master course content, students nevertheless seek us out for advice on how to improve their grades. Sharing with students study techniques we used when in school may or may not be helpful for struggling students (Lenze & Dinham, 1999, as cited in Wankat, 2002, p. 172). Since many professors were strong students, they may be at a loss when it comes to assisting an unprepared or at-risk student.

In college, one major problem for students who are experiencing academic difficulty is that they often try to study and organize their work the same way they did in high school, and the high school methods are usually not sufficient for college (Light, 2001, p. 37). College professors expect low-performing students themselves to discover new ways to study and organize, but all too often this expectation is too general and fails to offer specific strategies to help students actually find effective and efficient ways to study. For at-risk students, the trial-and-error method of finding new ways to study is not beneficial, and if they do figure out techniques that help, it may be too late. Academic dismissal frequently occurs before new study techniques are realized by the unprepared or at-risk student.

Introducing students to specific learning styles is an excellent way to help students analyze how they study and to increase their self-awareness and knowledge of the effectiveness of different types of study techniques. Most importantly, introducing specific learning styles encourages students to be responsible for their own learning. A major step in helping academically at-risk students is for them to accept this responsibility. In fact, all students who enroll in our class can probably improve on their ability to be responsible for their own learning. The process "involves developing intellectual maturity, learning skills, and awareness necessary to function as independent, autonomous learners" (Weimer, 2002, p. 95). We should and need to contribute to and be involved in this process, even though we may not previously have been very intentional about it (Weimer, 2002).

A quick, yet effective, way to become involved in the process is to assign students to take a formal learning styles inventory and then have them write about (or discuss) the results and different types of study techniques that complement preferred learning styles. The concern about the time that this might take away from the course content is allayed if students complete learning styles inventories as a homework assignment. After that, only a small amount of class time is needed to reinforce the importance of discovering and analyzing different learning or study strategies. No matter what subject is taught, a learning styles inventory can be used as supplementary material. As Weimer (2002) points out,

> Supplementary materials are the most common way faculty work on skill and awareness development. They are favorites because they can be assigned for working on out of class and therefore do not take class time away from content. I advocate using supplementary materials because good supplementary materials can support your work on developing learning skills and awareness by underscoring what is already an in-class priority and by helping make students responsible for their own development. (p. 58)

I recommend introducing learning styles to students right away. The earlier in the semester this is done, the better.

To begin, first give students a clear and simple definition of learning styles. For example, we can give them this fairly simple definition: "The term learning style refers to individuals' characteristic and preferred ways of gathering, interpreting, organizing, and thinking about information" (Davis, 1993, p. 185). When sharing this definition with students, I highlight the words *preferred ways* and point out that students can use less-preferred ways to learn and even develop their ability to use them. After a brief discussion about what learning styles are, I assign students to take a learning styles inventory, which will give them feedback on their learning style preferences. Several models of inventories that are available online are discussed in the next section. After taking one (or more) of the learning styles inventories, have students write or discuss their results. When analyzing their own preferred learning style, students can also investigate different types of study techniques that match their learning style preferences. Thus, learning styles can be used as a platform we can use to lead students to discover and build a repertoire of study strategies that can help them change the way they study and prepare for class.

Online Learning Styles Inventories

Of all the different types of learning styles inventories and models I have used with my students, my favorite is the *Index of Learning Styles Questionnaire* developed by Richard Felder and Barbara Soloman (1991) at North Carolina State University. It can be accessed at http://www.engr.ncsu.edu/learning styles/ilsweb.html. The questionnaire includes 44 phrases, or dependent clauses, with two possible independent clauses to complete the sentence. Students must choose the one that best describes themselves. For example,

I understand something better after I
(a) try it out.
(b) think it through.

I tend to
(a) understand details of a subject but may be fuzzy about its overall structure.
(b) understand the overall structure but may be fuzzy about details.

When I am learning something new, it helps me to
(a) talk about it.
(b) think about it.

(Felder & Soloman, 1991)

At the end of the inventory, students submit their answers for automatic scoring. A profile sheet of the student's learning style preferences is available for printing, along with a description and explanation of the results. The Felder and Soloman model has four scales with two learning style dimensions on each scale: (a) active or reflective, (b) sensing or intuitive, (c) visual or verbal, and (d) sequential or global. Each dimension can be briefly described as follows:

1. Active learners learn by trying things out and working with others [but] reflective learners learn by thinking things through, and working alone;

2. Sensing learners prefer information that is concrete, practical, and oriented toward facts and procedures [while] intuitive learners prefer information that is conceptual, innovative, and oriented toward theories and meanings;

3. Visual learners remember best what they see—pictures, diagrams, flow charts, time lines, films, and demonstrations. Verbal learners get more out of words—written and spoken explanations;

4. Sequential learners are linear, orderly, and learn in small incremental steps [whereas] global learners are holistic, systems thinkers and learn in large leaps. (http://www4.ncsu.edu/unity/lockers/users/f/felder/public/ILSdir/styles.htm by Felder & Solomon, n.d.).

For each scale, the student's score can range from 1 to 11, indicating whether the student is fairly well balanced on the two dimensions (scores of 1 to 3), has a moderate preference for one dimension (scores of 5 to 7), or has a strong preference for one dimension (score of 9 to 11). Once students have their results of the inventory, they can print out the descriptions for each scale to determine if they agree with their profile results.

On the Web site, Felder also provides a list of different study strategies that complement each dimension. I ask students to write an essay about their inventory results and the strategies that are suggested for their preferred style. Students must also include in their essay whether they agree with their individual results, and which of the study strategies they have tried or are willing to try. To reinforce this outside class assignment, we devote some class time to discuss their written reports. This activity can take as little as 10 minutes of class time.

Another example of an online inventory for learning styles is *The Learning Style Assessment* developed by Mencke and Hartman (2000). See http://www.ulc.arizona.edu/learning_style.php.

This questionnaire consists of 27 statements. The following are four of the statements on the assessment:

If I sat near a window in a classroom, I would probably be distracted by it.
I remember material better when I summarize it out loud.

I learn to spell better by reading a word out loud than by writing it on a
  paper.
I understand and follow directions on maps.
(Mencke & Hartman, 2000)

Students have three response choices for each statement: often, sometimes, or seldom. Once they respond to all the statements, they submit their
answers for immediate scoring and a results screen is displayed. Students
receive a score for three learning modes: visual (learn best by seeing), auditory (learn best by hearing), and kinesthetic (learn best by doing, by moving
physically, or by participative experiences). Study strategies for each of the
three learning modes are suggested for note taking, reading, exam preparation, and test taking. A more in-depth learning styles profile can also be
generated at this site.

As with the inventory by Felder and Soloman (1991), it is imperative
that students try the various ways to approach mastering course content to
get the full benefit of exploring their learning styles. "Many students have
never been exposed to . . . different ways to approach studying or even to
the idea that there are different ways to study. We can help students learn
about different strategies and when to use them" (Svinicki, 2004, p. 124).
When professors share strategies mastering specific material in their courses,
students can use or adapt those strategies to match their preferred learning
style.

A third example of a learning styles inventory is the VARK Questionnaire (Fleming, 2001–2006, at http://www.vark-learn.com/english/index
.asp). There are several links at this site, including a learning styles inventory
especially for athletes. The questionnaire can also be printed out if a professor wishes to have the students take the inventory during class hours. Once
students respond to all the questions, they can check the submit button, and
the scores are reported on a page titled "The VARK Questionnaire Results."
The five categories of different learning styles for this inventory are visual,
aural, read/write, kinesthetic, and/or multimodal learning preference. The
site also has a link to a list of strategies that apply to various learning preferences under different types of conditions.

The study strategies that are offered on these three Web sites can empower students. "In order for learners to control their learning, they need to be aware of available alternatives. Too many students come to college knowing only one or two strategies, which they use regardless of the task's demands. When those strategies don't work, the students simply try to do them harder rather than changing tactics" (Svinicki, 2004, p. 129). By introducing students to learning styles and various learning strategies, students will have new strategies to try. With new ways to tackle their learning tasks, at-risk students may have new hope (or confidence) in themselves as learners.

When teaching learning styles to my freshman class for at-risk students, I found many students were able to change the way they studied and, in turn, to change the outcome of their grades. One student in particular had a tremendous turnaround in her psychology class. The psychology course had a reputation for having a low success rate, and when Jamie came to see me with her F grade on the first midterm, I suggested that we look at her learning styles inventory results and how she had studied for the test. For the second midterm, she used new study strategies that were suggested, and although she was apprehensive, she earned a C. Her confidence in her learning ability changed dramatically, and on the next test grade she improved further, receiving a B. Her improvement was typical of most at-risk students I have worked with. Even though her teacher was a traditional "stand-and-deliver" lecturer, Jamie was able to change the way she studied and find success. For many students, "understanding learning styles will help . . . [them] cope with teachers whom they see as difficult" (Wankat, 2002, p. 183).

When discussing learning styles, ask students what environmental factors, especially in class, add to or detract from their learning. Ask the students, "What circumstances might add to or detract from your efforts or concentration when you are gathering and processing information?" Then, ask the students to write down at least two or three things. After collecting data from students for over 4 years, I have found that "distractions" (such as side chatting by other students, door banging by students who are tardy or who leave early, cell phones ringing) are the number one factor students give that have a negative impact on their learning. Poor lighting and an inability to hear the professors' voice are the next highest responses.

During this exercise I ask students, "What do you have control of in a class? What actions can you take to increase your learning focus or to avoid things that take away from your learning?" These questions eventually lead to interesting and obvious comments and solutions. For example, some students respond to those who say that being hungry or cold in class keeps them from being able to pay attention with comments such as, "Have a snack before class," "Bring a granola bar to class," "Bring a sweater to class." This may seem like an oversimplified approach, but as we move to the more serious comments, I use this discussion as a basis to set ground rules for the class.

Once we get a consensus about creating a class climate that will be conducive to learning, students are reminded that they need to be responsible for their behavior and their learning. Furthermore, I add that using the information from their learning styles inventories (including the study suggestions) is expected.

Another factor that can affect students' learning styles is the discipline, or type of subject matter, that is being taught. Since learning style preferences may change from one subject to another, it is also an excellent idea to encourage students "to value different kinds of learning styles" and to study with students who have different learning styles than themselves so that "they can enrich their learning experiences and develop new strengths by working with a variety of learners" (Davis, 1993, p. 190). For example, Dwayne was a student of mine who arrived at college unprepared. He was the first person in his family to go to college and a minority student on a white-majority campus. His experience is an excellent illustration of how students can benefit from analyzing learning preferences and using the information to change the way they prepare for exams.

Dwayne had excellent class attendance, his own class notes, and backup class notes (an accommodation for his learning disability awarded by the disabled student services counselor). In tutoring sessions, he had taken reading notes and made more than 80 concept flash cards for the test. However, when he received his graded test, he had earned a D. Although he was very discouraged, he met with the professor to go through his incorrect answers.

The professor discovered that Dwayne *did* know a lot of the material when discussing it, but when reading the questions silently, he was incorrectly reading several of the questions and possible multiple-choice answers, which led him to mark the wrong answer. His test-taking strategies and study strategies complemented his learning style preferences but did not prepare him for the actual test situation. We discussed additional ways that he should study and constructed sample tests for him to practice on. Many of the test questions we made up included the types that he had missed, such as ones with double negatives: "All of the following except what are not part of the _____ theory?" In tutoring sessions, which had focused on his verbal learning style, he practiced reading silently and using visual cues to complement his preferred auditory learning style. For the next two midterms, Dwayne's test performance improved significantly.

Dwayne's situation is an excellent reminder that learning strategies and styles are "responses and attitudes" that are learned. As Svinicki (2004) points out, they can be "unlearned or relearned. . . . They also can be used strategically—that is, truly flexible students can learn an array of strategies that allow them to cope with all the different kinds of situations they encounter" (p. 193). Having an array of useful learning strategies can be the difference maker for at-risk students.

Learning Styles and Learning Approaches

When considering learning styles, it is also worthwhile to consider how learning styles relate to research on *deep* and *shallow* learning approaches. Since the concepts of deep and shallow learning are new to most students, we begin with definitions of shallow (or surface) and deep learning approaches that are used when reading academic textbooks. According to Marton and Saljo, surface learning occurred "when students concentrated on memorizing the facts, focused on the discrete elements of the reading, failed to differentiate between evidence and information, were unreflective, and saw the task as an external imposition" (as cited in Weimer, 2002, p. 11).

On the other hand, Marton and Saljo described deep learning as, "when students focused on what the author meant, related new information to what they already knew and had experienced, worked to organize and structure the content, and saw the reading as an important source of learning" (as cited in Weimer, 2002, p. 11). Even though the formal definitions of deep and surface learning are new to most students, when I discuss examples of the two styles of processing new information, they say that often the kind of assignments they are given do not require a "deep" approach.

In her research, Svinicki (2004) found that "students with a surface processing approach to learning tend to use learning strategies that emphasize repetition and practice" (p. 198). However, even if surface learning is a preference for many students, they can be encouraged to use deep learning approaches by the actions of the teacher (p. 201). Svinicki explains,

> When the big picture focuses on relationships among main ideas, students are encouraged to process information at a deeper level, which is better in the long run. Whatever an instructor can do to encourage deep processing in all the students will pay off with longer retention and better understanding. (p. 201)

As teachers, we can promote deep learning by

1. Having students create concept maps or outlines where parts of a concept relate to another part,
2. Having students organize new information into meaningful patterns that reflect the underlying structure of the concepts that are being taught, or
3. Having students elaborate on concepts by "adding details and information that connect new information to prior knowledge." (Svinicki, 2004, p. 198)

By developing assignments that require surface and deep learning, in class and out of class, we can help students develop and expand their learning styles and strategies.

In another study conducted by Biggs, Kember, and Leung (2001), students who were deep learners adjusted their learning style to take a surface approach when enrolled in a class that covered a great deal of material and tested students' knowledge with multiple-choice tests that stressed detailed information. For students who are not deep learners, and/or are also at risk, making adjustments for a specific class may be difficult. However, as their teachers, we can help them make the connections so that they choose the appropriate learning approach for different types of exams and other assignments. By doing this, we are also helping them improve their chances of success.

Learning Styles and the Science of Learning

As a complement to the investigation of learning styles and learning approaches, it is also helpful to share with students some of the research findings on how people learn. In their article "Applying the Science of Learning," Halpern and Hakel (2003) discuss 10 "basic laboratory-tested principles drawn from what we know about human learning" (p. 38). My favorite five to discuss with my students are

1. What and how much is learned in any situation depends heavily on prior knowledge and experience.
2. Learning is generally enhanced when learners are required to take information that is presented in one format and "re-represent" it in an alternative format.
3. Varying conditions under which learning takes place makes learning harder for learners but results in better learning.
4. The single most important variable in promoting long-term retention and transfer is practice at retrieval.
5. Learning is influenced by both students' and our own [the professors'] epistemologies. (pp. 38–39).

When presented with these five principles, students are asked to consider what they can do with this information. For example, I will say, "How can you assess your prior knowledge and understanding at the start of an instructional unit (or unit of study)? Before reading a chapter or going to class, consider what you already know about the subject." We take a few chapter titles from the text I use in my course and also use texts from other courses. The exercise helps students practice how to assess their own prior knowledge and experience in several subjects.

For the principle of re-representing information, I give the students some information in a text (paragraph) format, and with a partner, they have to re-represent the information and share it with the class. Students are usually surprised and amused to see the variety of diagrams, pictures, and/or charts their classmates create. For the next three principles, students discuss and present their ideas on how to use and apply the principles in their study habits and routines. Also, through the semester, I often refer students to their learning styles results and the science-of-learning principles. In particular, for practicing retrieval of information, we demonstrate or explain to students different ways they can accomplish this.

Benefits for Professors

Having students investigate different types of learning styles and various complementary learning strategies can also benefit faculty members in several ways. Specifically, most faculty members who understand learning styles and orientation will (a) seek to expand and improve their teaching methods, (b) develop flexible grading (or assessment) methods that increase accuracy of measuring what students are learning, and (c) expand their methods to inspire their students to learn and master the course content.

Professors who have their students take a learning styles inventory and write about the results usually become aware of the variety of learning styles that exist among their students, and they analyze their own teaching style. Faced with diverse student learning styles, we must expand and improve our teaching style and methods.

Chickering and Gamson (1987) include as one of the seven principles of good practice "respects diverse talents and ways of learning" (p. 1). We can accommodate this principle by making sure that we develop a variety of approaches for our courses. Teaching activities may include, but are not limited to, short lectures, demonstrations, problem-solving tasks, in-class group work, individual in-class work, in-class discussions, and use of visual material including PowerPoint slides and overheads.

In their research, Kuh et al. (2005) discovered that "many more students would excel by [professors] using different combinations of teaching approaches and learning conditions" (p. 302). It is impossible to try to match every student's learning style since there will be a wide variety in any given class. However, by expanding and diversifying one's approach—beyond the traditional stand-and-deliver lectures—we can change a classroom climate in positive ways. "Understanding the difference can help professors plan more effective teaching strategies and help students become more effective learners" (Wankat, 2002, p. 172). In my discussions with many professors, most have said that recognition of learning styles often becomes a first step in embracing learner-centered teaching.

Acceptance of different types of learning styles and various complementary learning strategies also leads to the realization that not only do students benefit from a variety of instructional methods and learning activities, but they also benefit when they have the opportunity to demonstrate what they are learning in a variety of ways. This has led many instructors to develop flexible grading (or assessment) methods that increase accuracy of measuring what students are learning. When it comes to grades, Wankat (2002) offers the following advice: "Generally speaking, the more scores you have, the more accurately the final grade will reflect student learning" (p. 89). In addition, the more ways that students have to show what they are learning—not just their performance on tests and quizzes—the better they will perform. Flexible assessment benefits both faculty effectiveness and student learning:

> Alternative evaluation techniques—such as project and portfolio-based assessments instead of test-based—permit many students who have been frustrated in the traditional educational environment to demonstrate what they know and can do. Moreover, these approaches foster their learning (Kuh et al., 2005, p. 204).

It makes perfect sense to set up multiple ways that students can demonstrate what they are learning and to weave in assessment of what students are learning as the semester goes along (see chapters 7 and 8 for further discussion). In particular, when faculty allow students to demonstrate their learning by writing papers, completing projects, making presentations, or solving problems in addition to taking tests, students with diverse learning styles are supported and allowed "to build from their strengths" (Kuh et al., 2005, p. 32). Professors should avoid evaluating and grading student learning only by exams. Furthermore, at-risk students should avoid classes where exams (including quizzes, midterms, and final tests) are the only way they are graded. More than any other population at the university, unprepared students can improve and learn when they have a variety of ways to demonstrate what they are learning.

A third benefit faculty discover from introducing their students to learning styles is that it opens up new ideas and methods for inspiring students to learn and master the course content. Faculty who understand and appreciate learning styles can increase their effectiveness and their students' productivity (Davis, 1993, p. 185). Kuh and associates (2005) agree and add the following conclusion from their research: "Recognizing students' talents and preferred learning styles empowers them and also makes it possible to raise standards for academic challenge" (p. 205).

Conclusion

When at-risk students learn about learning styles, learning approaches, and concepts from the science of learning, and use the information to select and expand their study strategies, their learning power can be increased. Faculty can guide students to the information, but ultimately it is the students' responsibility to embrace and use it. Along with this increased learning power of their students, faculty will also benefit from widening and improving their pedagogical methods. It is important that students are given the "opportunity to show their talents and learn in ways that work for them" (Chickering & Gamson, 1987, p. 6). Having diverse methods for learning and teaching is beneficial for all students, but extremely worthwhile for academically at-risk students. Knowledge of learning styles and various complementary strategies can not only empower students, but it can also increase students' sense of responsibility in the learning process.

6

EMBRACING LEARNER-CENTERED EDUCATION

Engaging Students

The mere imparting of information is not education. Above all things, the effort must result in
making a man think and do for himself.

—Carter G. Woodson

Professors often ask me, "What can I do to make a difference with at-
risk students who are in my class?" My first response is, "Be a
learner-centered teacher." I tell them this because, more than any
other type of instructional model, learner-centered teaching engages students. Briefly, learner-centered education focuses on how students are learning the material and applying it, instead of traditional professor-centered
education, which focuses on how professors present information to the students, usually in a lecture format.

Kuh et al. (2006) point out the importance of student engagement for
at-risk students. In their research, they examined the results of students
engaged in effective educational practices and found that those who started
college with lower ACT and SAT scores and lower high school grade point
averages showed greater improvement in their college grades and higher persistence rates than the students who started college with higher entry scores.
While the more prepared students also improved in learning-centered environments, the ones who showed the largest improvement were the at-risk
students (Kuh et al., 2007).

Some emerging research suggests the engagement may have compensatory effects for at-risk students, including low income, first generation, and students of color attending PWI [predominately white institutions]. These findings suggest that seeking ways to channel student energy toward educationally effective activities would be wise, especially for those who start college with two or more "risk" factors. (Kuh et al., 2006, p. 48)

The potential to have all our students improve is reason enough to embrace learner-centered education methods, but when considering the dramatic impact that we can have on at-risk students, even the skeptics and the naysayers might be convinced to reconsider how students are engaged in their classes. Still, when I suggest shifting to learner-centered teaching, I see the worried look in many professors' eyes. Their biggest concern appears to be this: They do not know exactly what kind of changes they should make to implement this shift.

In the field of learner-centered teaching, some take an extreme approach, suggesting that the role of the teacher is minimal and that students should select topics and evaluate their own work with teachers giving little to no guidance (Wankat, 2002, p. 60). In my view, professors who take such an extreme approach to student- or learner-centered pedagogy go too far toward giving students total control and usually also end up with "limited effectiveness" (Wankat, 2002, p. 61).

In 1995 Barr and Tagg wrote about a new teaching paradigm in undergraduate education, describing the shift of the focus from "[professor- or] content-centered to learner-centered" teaching (p. 12). They describe content-centered professors as those who focus on sharing facts and concepts primarily through lectures and reading assignments. On the other hand, learner-centered professors focus on "how students think by emphasizing active learning strategies" (McKeachie, 2002, p. 285). Learner-centered teachers ask, "How are learners thinking, using, and applying the content?" Weimer (2002) adds,

In a learner-centered environment, content and learning are thought of as mutually reinforcing. . . . [first we use] active learning, that large repertoire of strategies and techniques designed to involve and engage students. Active learning is not a set of tricks to use with basically bored students. It is a powerful tool with well-established results. Those results, however, accrue only when active learning strategies involve content. Whatever it is that students are doing should involve legitimate, bona-fide course content. (p. 53)

At this point, some readers may be reflecting on their own college education where the lecture method was the most predominant paradigm of instruction. Teachers did most of the talking, and students sat passively, listening and taking notes. We know that we did learn from that method. However, as Huba and Freed (2000) note, "traditional, teacher-centered methods are 'not ineffective, . . . but the evidence is equally clear that these conventional methods are not as effective as some other, far less frequently used methods'" (Terenzini & Pascarella, 1994, p. 29, as cited in Huba & Freed, p. 2). By using learner-centered teaching methods, we design environments that "can optimize learning" (Bransford, Brown, & Cocking, 2000, p. 23).

The main differences between traditional content-centered teaching and learner-centered teaching can be shown in the planning process. For professors who are content centered, their teaching focus is on what the teacher will do (i.e., preparing the lecture, selecting visuals, deciding what demonstrations might be performed and handouts or reading to be assigned). With learner-centered teaching, the focus shifts to the students and the learning process. As teachers, we ask the following types of questions: What do my students already know about the subject matter/content? What will they be doing with the content? How can students practice what they are learning? What kind of activities or projects can students do that will help them grasp the new information and integrate it with their prior knowledge?

It is not that lecture is never used in a learner-centered environment; rather, the lecture is simply not the only thing that we plan for our classes. "Learner-centered teaching does not prohibit lecturing. . . . Lecturing becomes one of many possible methods, all evaluated on the basis of their ability to promote appropriate learning" (Barr & Tagg, 1995, p. 14). Furthermore, our new methods include active and collaborative pedagogies, "where learning is the focus and ultimate goal of the learner-centered paradigm. Because of this, assessment plays a key role in shifting to a learner-centered approach" (Huba & Freed, 2000, p. 8). How will we, the teachers, assess and evaluate students' learning and success? How can we help them evaluate their own learning? With the learner-centered approach, the "professor's role is to coach and facilitate," intertwining teaching and assessment, and "professors and students learn together" (Huba & Freed, 2000, p. 5; see chapters 7 and 8 for further discussion).

Defining Student Success

In order to evaluate student success, we must first define it. Kuh et al. (2006) broadly define student success as "academic achievement, engagement in educationally purposeful activities, satisfaction, acquisition of desired knowledge, skills and competencies, persistence, attainment of educational objectives, and post-college performance" (p. 7). They also point out that the use of effective teaching methods is at the core of any agenda promoting students' success (p. 66). Teaching methods that engage students in meaningful educational activities are the most effective. Collaborative learning, team-based learning, classroom-based problem solving, and service learning are a few examples of learner-centered teaching methods that actively engage students.

Since we know that all students, including at-risk and unprepared students, learn more in learner-centered environments, we must embrace this type of pedagogy and introduce it to our students during the first week of class (see chapter 3 for further discussion). We can do this verbally in class, but we should also have it in writing in our course syllabus, along with clear learning outcomes listed, an up-front and understandable grading system, and a list of the expectations we have of our students regarding their responsibility for their own learning and for classroom etiquette.

Encouraging and Clarifying Student Responsibility

Learner-centered education promotes classroom community and at the same time individual responsibility for learning (Barr & Tagg, 1995, p. 6; Bransford, Brown et al., 2000; Huba & Freed, 2000; Nilson, 1998; Weimer, 2002).

Also, "it is important for faculty to have high aspirations for learning outcomes, clear expectations for student performance, and standards for holding students accountable" (Hassel & Lourey, 2005; Tagg, 2003 cited by Kuh et al., 2006, p. 67). Discussing each of these factors in class and writing about them in our syllabi can help us communicate more effectively with our students because our syllabus is "one of the very first impressions we give our students. . . . it is the one piece of evidence our students can hold in their hands at the end of a day filled with a jumble of confusion" (Baecker, 1998, p. 60).

Baecker (1998) proposes that we strive to be up front and honest on our syllabi by using the pronouns *I, we,* and *you* accurately and in a way that clearly describes who will be doing what and who is responsible for what. She notes that our syllabi are where all the "issues about power and authority come together," (p. 58) and, therefore, we need to use the pronoun *I* when we describe what we, as the teachers, will be doing. In her examination of 15 syllabi, Baecker found that most were "rife with contradictions" (p. 58), because teachers used the pronoun we when in fact it would not be the case. One example that Baecker presents is of a professor who writes, " 'We will increase our awareness of the intimate connections among writing, reading, speaking, and listening.' This, of course, is an instance of the false we, because it can be assumed that her awareness of the connections between writing, reading, and listening has already been developed" (p. 61). Baecker reminds us that when we attempt to achieve a sense of community in our classes, we cannot forgo individual responsibility or blur our lines of author- ity when it comes to how we will grade our students on their individual assignments. The following is an excerpt from a clear, well-written syllabus that has an example of the clarity Baecker proposes when we describe to students who should be doing what:

> Though the type of essay *you'll* write is predetermined, the topic is not. *You'll* have to perform research and properly cite sources. *I'll* score each essay according to how well it addresses the "basic features" of that type, as discussed in the text. (p. 60)

In addition to being clear about the expectation for grades, we need to be clear about class attendance and participation in educationally meaningful activities—both in and out of class.

Preparing for Resistance

When we describe to students our intentions for using in-class activities and projects that will engage them, some of our students will protest. Many students are used to being in college courses where the traditional lecture method is used, so when they first hear that active learning methods will be used during class time, some students will resist. They may suggest that it is "the professor's job" to tell them what they need to know and to deliver well-prepared lectures. Some students will even suggest that they have paid with their tuition dollars for their teachers to teach them. There are several ways to counter such resistance.

On the first day of class, we can give students the research on learner-centered teaching and let them see how it shows that it helps students learn more and understand better (Felder & Brent, 1996). A major misconception that some students have is in their definition of teaching—they believe somehow that teaching is something that can be done only by a professor. However, "Teaching is not something you can go into the forest and do by yourself" (Ralph W. Tyler, educator, 1902–1994). Students have to be involved and participate in the process.

A second step we can take to counter negative attitudes is to point out the connection between the skills that students develop in a learner-centered class and the skills that they can use in their future careers. For example, prospective employers want to hire people who know how to take responsibility for their learning and not those "who are willing to sit back and passively wait to be taught" (Resistance to Active Learning, 1995–1997).

A third step is to solicit the students' cooperation. Many professors tell their students that the success of a course depends on the students' "willingness to adopt an active learning mode." In addition to telling students this, it should be put in our syllabi and discussed several times throughout the semester.

Even if students initially resist, do not assume that this resistance will continue as students become involved in the learning process. When discussing the importance of students participating in meaningful educational activities, I explain to the students the "class activity points" (see chapter 4) and how they are part of the grading system.

At-risk and unprepared students may be worried about their ability, or inability, to work with other classmates and how they will be able to participate in class activities. To address this possible issue, we should first consider Bandura's (1994) work.

Bandura (1994) asserts that a person's beliefs in his or her own capabilities to produce designated levels of performance (also known as self-efficacy) will "determine how people feel, think, motivate themselves and behave" (p. 2). He also states that those with a strong sense of efficacy "approach difficult tasks as challenges to be mastered rather than as threats to be avoided. . . . In contrast, people who doubt their capabilities shy away from difficult tasks. . . . They slacken their efforts and give up quickly in the face of difficulties" (p. 2). Often, at-risk students will focus their energies and efforts on tasks they believe they can achieve and avoid tasks they feel offer no hope of success. Students who have been successful in extracurricular activities (e.g., sports, drama, band, sorority or fraternity groups) are particularly vulnerable to becoming off balance in college. For example, many at-risk student-athletes who succeeded in sports and struggled in school may have a tendency to give up on academic endeavors.

Bandura (1994) examines sources of self-efficacy, which include mastery experiences: "Successes build a robust belief in one's personal efficacy. Failures undermine it, especially if failures occur before a sense of efficacy is firmly established" (p. 2). He warns that people who experience only easy successes do not build resiliency. However, some minor failures may actually kindle growth: "Some setbacks and difficulties in human pursuits serve a useful purpose in teaching that success usually requires sustained effort" (p. 3). When people endure minor failures but persevere in order to ultimately attain success, they almost always emerge stronger at the end of the experience. Thus, for many at-risk students, once they experience some success in school, they become more confident in all their courses, even if there are minor failures in the beginning.

As mentioned throughout this book, giving students individual feedback on early assignments is especially important for at-risk students. "Waiting until midterm examinations is often too late to give students an idea of how well they are performing" (Kuh et al., 2006, p. 94; see chapter 8 for further discussion). By using formative assessments, feedback, and activities where students "practice" what they are learning, at-risk students have a chance to improve before being tested on their new knowledge and, thus, their confidence will improve (see chapter 7 for further discussion).

Resistance to learner-centered teaching may not just come from students, but it could also come from administrators, deans, or department chairs. Barr and Tagg (1995) relate this true incident:

> A biology instructor was experimenting with collaborative methods of instruction in his beginning biology classes. One day his dean came for a site visit, slipping into the back of the room. The room was a hubbub of activity. Students were discussing material enthusiastically in small groups spread out across the room; the instructor would observe each group for a few minutes, sometimes making a comment, sometimes just nodding approval. After 15 minutes or so the dean approached the instructor and said, "I came today to do your evaluation. I'll come back another time when you're teaching." (p. 16)

Since lecturing has been so ingrained in our institutions, this example illustrates that it is not just students who define teaching as lecturing. Many administrators, deans, department chairs, and fellow faculty may also.

Establishing a Learning Community

In describing specific purposes of the learner-centered paradigm, Barr and Tagg (1995) explain that another aspect of this model is "to create environments and experience that bring students to discover and construct knowledge for themselves, to make students members of communities of learners that make discoveries and solve problems" (p. 16). Students cannot develop a sense of community if they do not talk to each other, or if there is a constant coming and going of students. Students arriving midway through the class period (or even when one-fourth of the class time has elapsed) or leaving early disrupt the learning process for everyone else.

During the first week of class, when introducing the students to learner-centered teaching and also to individual learning styles (see chapter 5), I ask the students to participate in establishing ground rules for our class that will prevent disruption and maximize our learning environments. Inevitably, the students come up with the same set of ground rules that I would want: attend all classes, arrive on time, stay for the whole period, be respectful to each other. I have found that most of the students follow these expectations since we decided on them together and especially since they are actively engaged during class time throughout the semester. For the few students who do not comply, I talk with them individually as needed—either before or after class.

At the beginning of one semester I had a student, Adam, who arrived at least 10 minutes late every class. Because of this, he missed out on most of the group activity when we decided on ground rules. When I asked him to stay after class to talk to me, he told me that he was late because he was coming from another class that went over, and it was located on the other side of campus. I suggested that he drop my class if he could not arrive on time. When I got back to my office, I looked up his schedule on the SIS and discovered that he did not have a class immediately before the one I was teaching. Rather than confronting him with this information (after all, he could have added a class that was not in the SIS yet), I began the next class with an activity where everyone was put into small groups. When Adam arrived late, I told him he could not join a group late—directions were already given, groups had already been formed, and he would have to wait until the activity was over. I also informed him of the class activity points he had already missed out on from the previous classes, and that he had lost the opportunity to earn any points for the current class. That was the last time I had to talk to him about arriving to class on time—Adam was not late again.

This example of my dealing with Adam is an excellent reminder that we need to talk to our students and never ignore inappropriate behaviors—whether it is something small such as being tardy to class or missing class, or something more serious such as side chatting or having private conversations when someone else is talking (including me or another student). Any type of disruptive or disrespectful behavior must be addressed.

Because learner-centered environments involve significant interaction among the students, most professors who teach this way find that rude behaviors, such as sleeping in class, reading the newspaper, text messaging, listening to an iPod, or surfing the Internet, do not occur. These kinds of behaviors must not be tolerated. I tell students with such behaviors that they need to choose—either get involved in our class and cease the inappropriate behavior or drop the class. Follow-up is crucial—when students make the requested changes, I praise them. If not, I administratively drop them.[1]

The Prior Knowledge Factor: Meet Students Where They Are

Learner-centered education has many different aspects that must be integrated. Bransford et al., (2000) note, "We use the term 'learner centered' to refer to environments that pay careful attention to the knowledge, skills, attitudes, and beliefs that learners bring to the educational setting" (p. 134). What students already know is often referred to as *prior knowledge*.

Zull (2002) describes important ideas about prior knowledge that all teachers should pay attention to. He writes that "prior knowledge is a fact. . . . Learners do not begin with a blank slate, [and] prior knowledge is the beginning of new knowledge. It is always where all learners start. They have no choice" (p. 93). He points out that one of the major mistakes that we as teachers in higher education often make is starting ". . . where *we* are, not where *our students* are" (p. 103). He notes that our teaching will be hindered if we ignore prior knowledge.

---

[1] Disruptive or disrespectful behavior should not be confused with threatening behaviors. If you feel you or other students are threatened, call campus police immediately and contact your appropriate campus administrators. For more information on distinguishing these different types of behavior, contact your dean of students office or the appropriate campus department.

There are many ways we can assess our students' prior knowledge. Angelo and Cross (1993) have several classroom assessment techniques (CATs) specifically for assessing prior knowledge.[2] Zull (2002) also proposes that we can have our students write about their prior knowledge. He suggests that when presenting new material or content, we should begin with concrete specific examples since most students' prior knowledge is concrete (p. 109). At-risk students typically have less prior knowledge than their more prepared classmates. Thus, professors can intervene to help these students fill in the gaps by having them come during office hours or attend review sessions that begin with where the students currently are in their understanding and knowledge. In some cases, students need to take another class to prepare them for your class. By doing this, we are showing our students that we value what they bring to the setting and that we want them to succeed.

When students know that we value their diverse backgrounds and ethnic heritages, they will feel welcome in our class, and this feeling is important for sharing and working together. "In addition, when faculty honor and celebrate student backgrounds and encourage students to make use of their prior knowledge, they empower students as learners" (Kuh et al., 2005, p. 205). Creating an inclusive classroom for students with different ethnic heritages and backgrounds, perspectives, and hopes and dreams is very important in any type of learning environment, but it is absolutely required for learner-centered teaching. We cannot assume that somehow our students will meet, talk to each other, and get along. In his book, *Making the Most of College: Students Speak Their Minds*, Light (2001) points out how students from different subgroups have been exposed to

> different literature, different perspectives about societal institutions such as police protection and crime control, and different expectations about how the leadership of a college or university will treat them. These differences challenge everyone on campus to respond constructively. As long as students interact across groups both in classes and in situations of living,

---

[2] Background Knowledge Probe and Misconception/Preconception Check are two of my favorite CATs that I use for assessing the prior knowledge of my students. There are several more CATs in their text that professors can use and adapt for their courses (also see chapter 7 for further discussion of CATs).

working, studying and socializing, they can learn something different, something more. (p. 152)

Kuh et al. (2005) also discuss the importance of having a classroom environment (or climate) ". . . that encourages contact among students from different economic, social, and racial or ethnic backgrounds" (p. 219). They also recommend that professors have serious conversations with students of different ethnicities and with students who have different religious beliefs, political opinions, and values. These conversations are beneficial to the students and the professor by exposing each to unique backgrounds and differing beliefs.

In addition, I recommend that we look at the types of books that we have on our bookshelves, since what we read can also communicate a positive message to our students. When students come to our offices, many will notice the books we have collected. Of course, most assume that we will have books related to our specific disciplines. However, by including books (and of course reading books) by authors from a variety of ethnic backgrounds, we can let our students see that we are interested in different ethnic heritages. Although my background is white European American, I have read many books by authors who are Native American, African American, or Mexican American. I keep these books in my office so that my students from minority backgrounds can see that I am interested in the rich and wonderful diversity of our country.

In class I have several ways of mixing students so that when they work, they can meet new classmates (see Appendix C). By the end of the semester, everyone has had the opportunity to meet and work with all the other students in the class. I don't allow students to pick their own groups because when they do they usually just turn to whomever they happen to be sitting next to rather than change seats to meet other people in the class.

This thoughtful and intentional mixing of students is beneficial in several ways. First, students have a chance to work with people from different backgrounds. Second, instead of talking with the same people every class, which can lead to social loafing, students stay on task. At the end of the semester, students always tell me how much they enjoyed meeting and working with everyone in the class. Third, the planned structure of having different student groups ensures interaction and conversations among students with different ethnic heritages, religious beliefs, political opinions, and values—as recommended by Kuh et al. (2005).

In *How Minority Students Experience College*, Watson, Terrell, Wright, and Associates (2002) point out the importance of inclusion for minority students on PWIs:

> At the close of the day, most students really want to be part of campus life, [including the classroom]. Most just want to know that they can participate and that their participation will be recognized and appreciated. (p. 106)

As professors, we can plan for inclusion and help our students from different backgrounds and ethnicities meet and participate in meaningful educational activities together in a learner-centered environment.

Conclusion

For at-risk and unprepared students, taking courses taught by professors who are learner-centered teachers will give them a genuine and greater chance for success. The value of creating a learner-centered environment that maximizes student learning has been documented by several research studies covered in this chapter and throughout this book. Kuh et al. (2006) summarize the importance of learner-centered teaching best:

> This shift promises to have profound implications for setting higher expectations for students, for raising academic standards, for asking students to take more responsibility for their learning, for demonstrating competency through assessment, and for emphasizing and validating alternative ways of knowing, interdisciplinary methods, and problem-focused learning. (p. 66)

In addition, learner-centered education acknowledges students' prior knowledge and diversified backgrounds. Learner-centered teaching supports

Chickering and Gamson's (1987) principles of good practice. "Good practices hold as much meaning for professional programs as for the liberal arts. They work for many different kinds of students—white, black, Hispanic, Asian, rich, poor, older, younger, male, female, well-prepared, underprepared" (p. 2). As teachers, it is our responsibility to include the principles of good practice in any type of pedagogy we use.

7

INTERWEAVING ASSESSMENT AND TEACHING

Any Questions?

Aim at a high mark and you'll hit it. No, not the
first time, nor the second time. Maybe not the
third. But keep on aiming and keep on shooting
for only practice will make you perfect.

—Annie Oakley

L ecturing to students has been an accepted and widely used pedagogy
at colleges and universities for many years. Along with lectures, midterms and final exams have been the customary way to determine
what students have learned. Usually tests are given at the end of a series of
lectures and assigned readings, and the results are used to calculate grades.
As new material is being presented, in traditional settings, most professors
will check for understanding by simply asking students if they have any
questions.

"Does everyone understand?" is a question that we, as teachers, often
pose to our students at the end of a lecture. Sometimes a professor will ask,
"Do you all see the solution?" when referring to the problem he or she just
solved on the chalkboard. As professors pause and look around the room,
students usually remain silent. From personal observation and testimonials
from many professors, I have found that rarely will students (any student)
say, "No. I don't understand," or even ask a question. Once in a while, one
or two students will have a question, but most of the time students will just
nod their heads and remain quiet.

In fact, many students may think that they have grasped whatever the lecture covered when the class ends, but then later they discover they cannot reexplain or apply the information. As Svinicki (2004) points out, when hearing an excellent explanation or presentation some students may have "an illusion of comprehension. . . . The fluency of the expert [presenting the material] may give the listeners the illusion of understanding or the belief that the material is clear and easy to understand" (p. 117). Students leave the class thinking that they know the material, when in reality they do not.

Conversely, some students do not have an illusion of comprehension, and they know that they have questions but are reluctant to ask them in front of their classmates. Many unprepared or at-risk students will say, "I didn't want to sound stupid in front of everybody." Others have told me, "I didn't know exactly what to ask. I really didn't understand the whole thing, but I thought I would be able to figure it out later." So, they say nothing.

When midterms are graded, we may be disappointed when many of our students perform poorly. Professors and students may also be frustrated, barring those instructors who are consoled if a few students perform well. At-risk students are rarely the ones who pass with flying colors. At-risk students are vulnerable since many either have suffered "illusions of comprehension," or were unwilling (or unable) to ask questions in or outside of class. When the first midterms are returned, it is not unusual for at-risk students to be surprised by their poor test performances and then to become dismayed and give up. One of my at-risk students, Chancy, came back to the support center after a failed exam and said to me, "Why study? I failed anyway."

Universities and colleges have responded to increasing numbers of students performing poorly in their classes by expanding learning centers and tutoring labs. While these additions can be very supportive for at-risk students, they are not enough. We need to participate in, and indeed actively supplement our institutions' efforts by adding assessment activities to our lectures and to our classrooms, and not wait until the midterm or other exams to find out how the students are doing. By using assessment techniques with greater frequency, not only will we gain feedback on how our students are progressing, but so will the students. Students and professors can then consider adjustments, interventions, and strategies to correct the situation.

Summative and Formative Assessment Differences

Summative assessments, such as midterms and finals, are ways to measure "what students have learned at the end of some set of learning activities" (Bransford et al., 2000, p. 140). Tests, term papers, quizzes, and other graded assignments are also traditional types of summative assessments that are regularly used to determine the students' grades. On the other hand, formative assessments, which have been used much less, are given in between summative assessments. The main purpose of formative assessments is to act as "sources of feedback to improve teaching and learning. Examples of formative assessments include teachers' comments on work in progress, such as drafts of papers, or preparations for presentations" (Bransford et al., 2000, p. 140).

Summative assessments, such as tests, also provide feedback but in a different sense. They are given at the end of the unit or lesson, and if students perform poorly, they can only hope to do better on the next test or assignment, which will most likely cover new material. Furthermore, most at-risk students do not know what to do with a failed test. Nathan, one of my unprepared students with a learning disability, had a reaction to a failed test that was typical of many at-risk students. When he came back to the support center, I asked him to go over the test with me so we could figure out what he had done wrong. He told me, "I don't have it. I felt so bad and I was so mad, I just threw it in the garbage." Thus, the opportunity to see if he had prepared incorrectly, misread questions, or just misunderstood the concepts or content was missed.

On the other hand, when formative assessments are used, students are taught to use the feedback on their performance so they can make improvements before they have to take the test or turn in the paper. Using formative assessments throughout the entire semester can make a powerful and significant difference in student learning. Students are able to demonstrate what they are learning. This is especially true for at-risk and unprepared students.

Huba and Freed (2000) believe that all assessments are "best when used to improve subsequent learning" (p. 8). When students have an opportunity to make corrections, rework problems, rewrite drafts, or reanalyze, the learning and the understanding of what is being taught are improved. At the same time, by conducting assessments, "We force the questions, 'What have our students learned and how well have they learned it?' 'How successful have we been at what we are trying to accomplish?'" (p. 8). Thus, the assessments that we use in our classes must be tied to the intended learning outcomes that we develop for our courses (see chapter 4 for further discussion). Furthermore, we can adjust our teaching as we receive information about our students' learning (Nilson, 1998, p. 176).

The results of the assessment activity can give the teacher valuable information on how the students are doing, but students must also receive individual feedback in order for the assessment activity to be effective and beneficial for them. All students can benefit from assessment activities, but at-risk students in particular benefit because frequent assessment and feedback helps *them* monitor their own progress more closely. Two major obstacles for unprepared, at-risk students are (a) lack of study strategies and (b) not being able to differentiate between essential and nonessential information. When these students are in classes where formative assessments are used in addition to summative assessments, their academic performance is enhanced and improved.

Another message that we teachers pass on to our students when we interweave formative and summative assessments throughout the semester is that we are demonstrating interest in our students' progress. When that happens, most students are motivated to do better. Monitoring students' progress in turn provides feedback on teaching methods and formats and opportunities to adjust them. "Designing and assessing student learning outcomes can lead to more responsive pedagogy" (Kuh et al., 2005, p. 205). That is, we as faculty can also adjust our teaching methods or formats if students do not comprehend the material. Note that this is not the same as lowering standards. Formative assessments help students meet high expectations.

Examples of Formative Assessment Techniques

In the film *Declining by Degrees: Higher Education at Risk* (Merrow & Tulenko, 2005), science professor Tom Fleming demonstrates an informal type of assessment activity when he posts a multiple-choice question on a PowerPoint slide. What the film does not show is when this assessment takes place, which is about 17 minutes after the class begins. He had been presenting material to the students (lecture style with visual aides), and then he posed a question to the class with a list of four possible answers. By using individual electronic response clickers, the students register their answers. On the PowerPoint slide, the responses are then added up, and the percentage of votes cast for each answer is shown (see Figure 7.1). After seeing the response totals, Fleming comments, "That's interesting. Most of you think that the answer is either C or D. So, I want you to talk to each other and convince your classmates why your answer is right." Next, the students talk to each other, and in a few minutes, Fleming asks them to vote again. This time, over 80% of the students have the right answer.

The engagement of the students is obvious to anyone watching the film. It is also important to note that most of the students got to the right answer without Dr. Fleming lecturing again or repeating himself. Furthermore, by being allowed to participate, students demonstrated energy and enthusiasm. They were involved in the learning process.

FIGURE 7.1
Example of Electronic Clicker Responses From Students

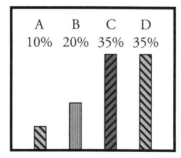

While it might be nice to have the electronic responders, those of us who do not have the technology available can still use the voting method to assess and engage our students. It is not as efficient at producing exact percentage results, but it still works and I have used it many times with great success. It is also very inexpensive, since it only requires the use of fluorescent-colored 3-x-5-inch cards. For true/false questions (or questions with two possible answers or opinions such as A or B), I use pink and green cards. Every student gets a green card and a pink card: green is for true (or choice A), and pink is for false (or choice B). When using these cards, students are instructed to show their votes simultaneously on the count of three after the question is read. Then the students raise their hands high with the card of their choice. All questions are on PowerPoint slides (or on an overhead transparency). After I pose the question, students vote. Looking around the room it is fairly easy for me to call out to the students who have not voted, or to those who try to hold up two cards, and ask them to decide. Then I estimate what the results are and say something like, "It looks like most of you voted false," or "About 70% are voting true, and 30% are voting false." We can then have the same kind of interactive discussion that Fleming had with his class. With a smaller class, students can tell the whole class why they voted a certain way. Of course, I ask for volunteers to explain their votes, and it is surprising how many students respond.

For multiple-choice questions, more colors can be added, such as fluorescent orange and yellow. A large answer code is placed in front of the room so that all the students can clearly see which color represents A, B, C, or D answers. This formative assessment activity is very informal, but it also gives students and the teacher immediate feedback.

A professor who tried out this assessment activity with her class of 92 students called me to report the results. She added an extra twist to the voting to get students talking to someone other than the people they had been sitting next to all semester. Once they voted, each student had to talk to someone who voted differently and try to convince that person why his or her vote was wrong. Students moved around the room to find a fellow classmate with a different vote. After a brief exchange, the professor had them vote again. Next, she randomly called on students to explain their final answer. At the end of the class, the professor reported the following:

> My lackluster class became invigorated. Everyone was involved. The critical thinking and application of the material was evident by the thoughtful answers and responses the students gave. At the end of the class, one student came up to me and said, "I wish all my classes were this interesting. I am learning so much. This is my favorite class and the best one I have ever had at this college. If only all of college could be like this!" (J. Borovay, personal communication, April 26, 2007).

Another assessment activity that many readers may be familiar with is "Write-Pair-Share" or "Think-Pair-Share." It is very easy to adapt and to use at the beginning, in the middle, or at the end of a class. Briefly, the activity involves three steps: (a) The instructor poses a question or problem, (b) students are given a specific amount of time to write down their responses, and (c) students are then paired with a classmate to discuss their answers. After students have a chance to talk with each other, the professor can call on a few students to share their answers with the entire class. I ask students to put their names on their written responses and pass them in. Usually students are given 3-x-5-inch cards to write on, but other times students just write answers on their own binder paper they have brought to class. By having students put their names on their answers, participation points can be awarded; it is also important for the teacher to read the students' responses. If the professor does not have time to write a short comment on each card, he or she should at least use a sign (+ +, +, —) that indicates that the student is on track or off track. Even a "Please see me (or the GA) for help" if the student really misses the point would be helpful.

Desrochers (1999) offers additional ways to elaborate on the Write-Pair-Share. She suggests that professors ask students for real-life examples, summarize key concepts from the lecture, "list cost and benefits or pros and cons, or diagram a process" (p. 1). Also, if the class is large and the noise level rises, professors should consider bringing a whistle or bell so they can signal the class when the time is up. Another technique that can be used to get the students' attention is to tell them that when the time is up, the professor will raise his or her hand. As soon as the students see a hand up, they raise their hand. All hands are to remain raised until the entire room is quiet. When using this technique, I have the class practice it before the sharing begins.

Write-Pair-Share can have a fairly quick impact on student engagement in one's course. For example, a professor contacted me for help with a general education course that was a lower-division requirement for majors in the field but also met a general education requirement. The professor was concerned about her students' passive, unresponsive, and lackadaisical behavior in general. She said that even when she asked for questions or comments, she got none. The class met every Tuesday and Thursday from noon to 1:15 P.M. The first time I observed her class, students came in on time and most of the seats were filled. The professor used slides to enhance and illustrate her lecture, and she dimmed the lights so the students could see the slides but have enough light to write notes. While not a dynamic or animated speaker, she was certainly not mundane or boring. It was obvious that she was enthusiastic about her subject. Her lecture was interesting, but 30 minutes into the class meeting, some students began sliding down in their seats. Some heads were bobbing, and some students were stretching as if to keep themselves awake. By the end of class, several students were not paying attention and appeared to be half asleep.

After class the professor and I discussed ways that she could use a formative assessment activity in the middle of her class to engage her students and assess how they were grasping the material. At the next class, after she had lectured for about 17 minutes, she stopped, turned the lights up, and explained the Write-Pair-Share activity. She gave them a question about the first part of her presentation and had students write their answers (with their names) on a 3-x-5-inch card. After they wrote their answers, she asked them to turn to a classmate to share and compare what they had written. Then she also asked several students to share their answers with the entire class.

The assessment activity took only about 5 to 7 minutes, but the class was energized. In addition, several students asked a few more questions. She then continued with the rest of her lecture. For the next class, she used the

Write-Pair-Share activity again. During the second half of the class, several students on their own accord raised their hands to make comments or ask questions. What a difference! After each class, she went through the cards and read their answers, made a short one- or two-word comment on each card, and returned them to the students.

For the rest of the semester, the professor continued to use this assessment technique and tried out a few others. She reported that her students continued to show their interest during class meetings, and on the next midterm, scores improved. The fourth time I visited the class, a few students in the back of the room approached me to ask if I had anything to do with the change that the professor had shown in her teaching methods. I jokingly replied, "Well, that depends. Do you like it?" With big smiles, they told me how much better the class was and said they had some other professors they wanted me to advise. The students who approached me were not at risk, but from their comments, one can see how using formative assessment techniques will break up the lecture and benefit all students.

The "Meta-Cognitive Moment" (Hester, 1998, p. 2) is another assessment technique that I have used with much success. Hester designed the Meta-Cognitive Moment to assess students' present knowledge "in order to connect new information to what they already know" (p. 2). The activity works as follows: After presenting information on a unit or topic, she puts "five simple analytical and synthesizing questions on the board" (p. 2). Questions can also be displayed on a transparency with an overhead projector or on a PowerPoint slide. Next, in small groups, students discuss what they think are the answers to the questions. I recommend three students per group, and absolutely no more than four. On an answer sheet, students write a simple "Yes" or "No" for each question. They do not write out the answer. Questions could be multiple choice or in essay form. For example, for an introduction to anthropology class, one question students might be given about marital residence and kinship is this:

In a matrilineal society, authority in the kin group is often exercised by

a. the mother's brother
b. the father's sister

    c. the oldest daughter

    d. the oldest son

The students in each group would discuss what they think the answer is, and if they all agreed on the answer, they would write "Yes" on their answer sheet, indicating that they all agreed that they know the correct answer. If not, they would write "No." An example of an essay question for an educational class on disabilities is: How are visual and hearing impairments defined, both legally and functionally? The students in each group discuss their answers and write "Yes" if they agree they know the answer, and "No" if they cannot agree on the answer or believe they are not sure if their answer is correct.

Hester gives her students about 10 minutes to discuss the answers and encourages anyone in the group who may know the answer to explain it to those who may not. Answer sheets with the names of the group members are turned in, and she discusses the "No" responses with the whole class, inviting other class members to help with the answer. As a result of this assessment activity, Hester is given relevant feedback on her students' comprehension of the material, and thus she can "explain again what has caused confusion" (p. 2). In addition, the students have a chance to "review information, which reinforces their knowledge of the material . . . [and] actively evaluate their own knowledge base" (p. 2). Hester also reports that as a result of the assessment activity, her students seem more confident and have less test anxiety.

When using the Meta-Cognitive Moment exercise, I have witnessed similar results. Furthermore, I also use it as a way to take roll and to evaluate class participation for that day. Circulating around the room, it is fairly easy to notice if anyone is not participating in the small-group discussion, which is rarely the case. Students appear to be comfortable in the small groups, and the vast majority review or add to their notes as they discuss their answers. This activity works well in the middle of a class period, but it can also be used at the beginning or toward the end. This activity is particularly helpful for at-risk students because they get a chance to see different types of test questions, and they have the opportunity to witness how their classmates review their class and reading notes and prepare for exams. From working with other students who are more prepared, at-risk and unprepared students will learn from their classmates how to improve their own study and test preparation skills.

To become acquainted with additional types of formative assessments that can be used during class time, an excellent source is *Classroom Assessment Techniques* by Angelo and Cross (1993). It is a practical handbook that includes 50 different classroom assessment techniques (CATs).

CATs are designed to involve teachers and students "in the continuous monitoring of students' learning" (Angelo & Cross, 1993, p. xiv) in a particular course throughout the semester. They should be used during class time and can take anywhere from 3 minutes to 20 minutes (or more), depending on how we adapt the particular assessment to our class and its context. The handbook is easy to use; for each assessment, there is a description along with its purpose, related teaching goals, suggestions on how to use the assessment, examples from various disciplines, and a step-by-step procedure.

Additionally, Angelo and Cross (1993) list ideas for adapting and extending each assessment technique. In my opinion, it is by far the best resource for professors and instructors, whether they are novices or experienced teachers.

The CATs are divided into three broad categories: (a) Techniques for Assessing Course-Related Knowledge and Skills; (b) Techniques for Assessing Learner Attitudes, Values, and Self-Awareness; and (c) Techniques for Assessing Learner Reactions to Instruction. In turn, each category has specific subsets with several different assessments to choose from. Probably the most widely known and used CATs are the Minute Paper and Muddiest Point. What all of the assessments have in common is that they actively engage students in a learning task and increase student-faculty interaction.

CATs are proven to be an effective education practice and by using them, at-risk students benefit more than any other type of student in our classes. In the words of George D. Kuh, director of the National Survey of Student Engagement, "When institutions use effective educational practices, they provide a small boost to students who are lower achieving when they start college. [For these students] the more engaged they become, the better their grades are, and they start catching up to students who started college with a higher level of achievement" (Wasley, 2006, p. A39).

Three of my favorite CATs, which I have found to be very engaging and helpful to all the students in my classes, are (a) the Memory Matrix, (b) What's the Principle? and (c) the Pro and Con Grid.

In classes that require students to memorize information, the Memory Matrix is an assessment that can be used in different ways. Angelo and Cross (1993) concisely describe the Memory Matrix as follows:

> [It] is a two-dimension diagram, a rectangle divided into rows and columns used to organize information and illustrate relationships. In a Memory Matrix, the row and column headings are given, but the cells, the boxes within, are left empty. When students fill in the blank cells of the Memory Matrix, they provide feedback that can be quickly scanned and easily analyzed. (p. 142)

Figure 7.2 shows a specific example of a filled-in matrix for an introductory psychology course. Figure 7.3 shows the Memory Matrix for Operant Conditioning that would be given to the students to fill in.

For courses with high informational content, this is a practical way to assess "student recall and basic comprehension of facts and principles"

FIGURE 7.2
Sample Matrix for Operant Conditioning

	Reinforcement		Punishment		
	Positive	Negative	Positive	Negative	
Repeatable Categories					
Behavior	Increase	Increase	Decrease	Decrease	DETAILS
Stimulus	Present	Remove	Present	Remove	

Adapted from *Learning to Learn: Making the Transition from Student to Life-Long Learner*, by K. Kiewra and N. Dubois, 1998, Boston: Allyn & Bacon.

FIGURE 7.3
Sample Memory Matrix for Operant Conditioning

	Reinforcement		Punishment		
	Positive	————	————	Negative	
Repeatable Categories					
Behavior					DETAILS
Stimulus					

(Angelo & Cross, 1993, p. 142). In particular, it can encourage at-risk students to re-represent information in a matrix form and help them recognize how and what they need to study before the summative exam. Students with stronger academic records may already be creating matrixes on their own, but unprepared students often have not used this valuable strategy. A variation of the activity is to have the students draw concept maps or create an organizational framework using a diagram or matrix. This exercise supports the basic principle from the science of learning, which states that learning is enhanced when learners are required to re-represent the information:

> Learning and recall are thus enhanced when learners integrate information from both verbal and visuospatial representations. . . . complex concepts can be related to one another in numerous ways, and depicting correct relationships among concepts is central to all graphic organizing techniques. . . . Faculty need to use both verbal and visuospatial processing activities in all of the learning tasks that they construct. (Halpern & Hakel, 2003, p. 39)

Thus, having students apply information to a memory matrix, or create their own organizational chart or diagram, can be used by the teacher as a formative assessment and by the student for learning the material. I remind all my students to use an empty memory matrix and practice completing it as they prepare for our unit tests. "If you have to look back at your notes, you are not ready for this part of the test" is a reminder I give all the students, but for at-risk students who never learn how to self-test in high school, this kind of advice is very helpful.

A second favorite CAT that I like to use with students is What's the Principle? in which students are asked to connect general principles to specific problems or practices. Angelo and Cross (1993) succinctly describe this CAT as follows:

> After students figure out what type of problem they are dealing with, they often must then decide what principle or principles to apply in order to solve the problem. This CAT focuses on that second step in problem solving. It provides students with a few problems and asks them to state the principle that best applies to each problem. (p. 218)

This CAT assesses students' skill in problem solving. We can create a form that is easy to score quickly. If the students have a lot of wrong answers, or if there are no sensible patterns, then they are probably guessing. However, recognizing problems and connecting principles to the problem may be something that less-prepared students will need to be explicitly taught how to do. This CAT will help us determine if we need to do that. If only a small group of students in the class need additional help, those students can go see the professor during office hours or the professor can hold a review session and require or invite the students to attend.

Angelo and Cross (1993) suggest several ways to adapt this CAT. One example is to ask the students to justify their choices of identified principles in a sentence or two. What I like best about this CAT is that it "promotes the learning of transferable problem-solving skills that students may remember long after they have forgotten specific examples" (p. 221).

The third CAT example I enjoy using with my students is the Pro and Con Grid. Angelo and Cross (1993) point out, "At one time or another, most people have jotted down quick lists of pros and cons to help them think more clearly about a pressing decision. This Pro and Con Grid turns that familiar decision-making exercise into a simple Classroom Assessment Technique with many possible applications" (p. 168). The Pro and Con Grid is also an excellent way for the professor and the students to determine if the students are prepared to participate in a class debate or write a compare-and-contrast essay. This kind of feedback is very helpful for at-risk students. At the same time, we can remind students who are not ready to participate that they will have to put in extra time in order to get ready.

Angelo and Cross (1993) point out that CATs are designed as formative assessments with the "purpose to improve the quality of student learning, not to provide evidence for evaluating or grading students" (p. 5). I agree; however, I grade the assessments but not in a traditional sense. I use the students' assessment responses as part of their class activity (or participation) points. Students can have wrong answers and receive full participation points for the day.

It is important to consider timing and pacing in using formative assessments to engage students during the class period, and indeed over the entire semester as it unfolds. When professors and instructors are continually lecturing to students, even if they are excellent and interesting speakers, they are the ones who are doing all the work. As we saw in the earlier example in this chapter, most students sit passively, listening and taking notes. Some may doze or daydream off and on. At best, the typical attention span for listening is no more than 20 minutes (Wankat, 2002, p. 68). However, when professors use formative assessment techniques throughout the class period, the students are obliged to interact and they have to make sense of the material and apply what they are learning. Formative assessments, as well as other types of meaningful educational activities, restart the student's attention span clock.

Conclusion

Lecturing and summative assessment have long been accepted pedagogical techniques at the college and university level, even though these techniques when used alone are not the most effective for promoting student learning. However, by interweaving formative assessment techniques into the class period, we can engage students and have them apply, analyze, synthesize, grasp, and transfer course concepts and content. Furthermore, professors and students can receive feedback on the learning processes, and what is being taught will be reinforced. If students are not progressing, they have a chance to get tutoring or seek additional help before a summative assessment is given. For at-risk students, this opportunity is beneficial for their success in college. Using the techniques described in this chapter can make a tremendous difference in helping unprepared students become competent college students.

8

TECHNIQUES FOR PROMOTING ACADEMIC INTEGRITY AND DISCOURAGING CHEATING

Playing by the Rules

Every problem contains the seeds of its own solution.

—Stanley Arnold

C heating is not just an at-risk student problem. Across college campuses in the United States, reports of academic dishonesty continue to cause alarm and concern faculty and administrators alike. These reports are not isolated incidents. In their extensive and comprehensive research studies, McCabe and Trevino (1996) found that 84% of the students surveyed admitted to some form of cheating as undergraduates. Furthermore, McCabe, Trevino, and Butterfield (2001) found that over the last 30 years, not only has the frequency of some forms of cheating incidents dramatically increased, but also the techniques (or methods) of cheating have expanded and become more sophisticated.

McCabe and Trevino (1997) report that lower-division students and students with lower grade point averages are more likely to cheat than students in upper-division classes and students with higher grade point averages. McCabe et al. (2001) also report that when deciding whether to cheat, the "contextual factors (peer cheating behavior, peer disapproval of cheating behavior, and perceived severity of penalties for cheating) were significantly

more influential than the individual factors (age, gender, GPA, and participation in extracurricular activities)" (p. 221). Thus, having a lower GPA is
probably less influential than other contextual factors. Nevertheless, when
focusing on at-risk or unprepared students, we must be aware that these
students may be more vulnerable or susceptible to cheating than other student groups if they have lower GPAs.

Over the last 5 years, I have conducted more than 30 workshops on
prevention of academic dishonesty. To begin each workshop, I ask participants to vote true or false on statements regarding research findings on student cheating, such as

> True or False: Males cheat more then females.
> True or False: Business and math majors report the most cheating
>   incidents.
> True or False: Younger students (lower division) cheat less than older stu-
>   dents (upper division).

All participants are given fluorescent cards (green for true and hot pink
for false) so that on my cue they can vote simultaneously true or false for
each statement. When I ask whether they think it is true or false that
McCabe and Trevino's (1997) research found that 84% of students admitted
to some kind of cheating as undergraduates, faculty groups will hold up an
array of pink and green cards. The vote is never more than 50% true. When
I ask the same question to student groups, they always vote 100% green
cards! When I ask why they voted that way, students say there is no doubt
in their mind this statement is true. "We know," the students tell me. The
only ones who seem surprised that the statement is true are professors.

When it comes to cheating, it is unclear if we professors are simply naive
or if we do not know how to deal with it. According to Mullens (2000), "A
sizable portion of faculty (32% in Dr. McCabe's February 2001 survey) who
were aware of cheating in their courses did nothing in response" (p. 26).
Some faculty decided not to report cheating incidents to the dean of students
(or the appropriate department), but instead handled it themselves by "failing the student on the test or assignment involved . . . a simple warning . . .
or various penalties less than test or assignment failure" (McCabe et al.,
2001, p. 223). When this happens, "word seems to travel quickly among

students as to who these faculty are, and students' comments suggest their courses become particular targets for cheating" (p. 223). Ignoring cheating or the potential of cheating should not be an option for any of us.

When examining how cheating should be handled, there are prevention techniques (discussed later in this chapter), but we cannot simply consider only these measures. "The best ways to reduce cheating are all about good teaching. In fact, if efforts to deal with cheating don't emerge from efforts to educate, they won't work, at least not when vigilance is reduced" (Stephens, 2004, p. 1). Many features constitute good teaching, but since cheating is usually associated with students trying to improve their grades, grading systems need to be examined first.

In college, professors will use either a criterion-referenced or norm-referenced grading system. When using criterion grading, the points (or percentages) that one needs for a certain grade are described. Each student's grade "reflects his or her level of achievement, independent of how other students in the class have performed" (Davis, 1993, p. 289).

On the other hand, with norm-referenced grades (also referred to as *grading on the curve*), "a student's grade reflects his or her level of achievement relative to other students in the class" (Davis, 1993, p. 290). With this kind of grading, students do not know if a score of 88% on a test will be an A, a B, a C, or even less. Only a certain proportion of the class can receive an A. Grading on the curve discourages students from studying together and "produces undesirable consequences for many students, such as reduced motivation to learn, debilitating evaluation anxiety, decreased ability to use feedback to improve learning, and poor social relationships" (p. 283). With this type of atmosphere, one cannot expect to build a trusting class environment, and it may lead to students taking "academic shortcuts" (McKeachie, 2002, p. 122).

"Academic integrity involves creating an ethos or culture of trust, responsibility, and honesty" (Herteis, 2003, p. 1). Thus, the first step to discourage cheating is to avoid norm-referenced grading and use criterion-referenced grading for all tests, quizzes, papers, projects, and so on in our courses. A criterion grading system works well with learner-centered teaching where "evaluation is used to generate grades and promote learning" (Weimer, 2002, p. 119). Everyone in the class has a chance to earn an A.

How grades are earned to make up the final grade should be clear and easy for students to calculate, so they can keep track of their progress throughout the semester. Thus, I recommend that the overall grading systems list point values along with percentages for the final grade (or grand total), as well as for the different projects, papers, or assignments that will make up the final grade. In the example in Figure 8.1, the point value for each category of graded assignments is listed along with each assignment's percentage value for the total grade. Students can add up the points they earn as the semester progresses, and they can check subtotals against the final grade breakdown, which is also listed with the percentage and point spread. Unless you and your students are well versed in math, giving only proportions, ratios, or weighted values will leave many students confused on exactly how their final grade will be determined.

Rubrics for Promoting Integrity

As previously mentioned in this book, having a variety of ways students can demonstrate what they are learning and having each activity directly related to the course's learning outcomes will promote learning and support the

FIGURE 8.1
Sample Grading System for the Entire Semester
With Percentage and Point Values

Components of the Semester Grade:	Percentage	Point Value
1) In-Class Activities (written responses, quizzes, etc.) ...	25%	100
2) Research Paper	20%	80
3) Written Reflections of Readings (8)	20%	80
4) Portfolio	5%	20
5) Midterm	12.5%	50
6) Final (required)	17.5%	70
TOTAL	**100%**	**400**

Points and Grading Scale for Final Grade

100%: (Criterion Grading)	90–100% A	360–400
	80–89% B	320–359
	70–79% C	280–319
	60–69% D	240–279

diverse learning styles and strengths of our students. It will also reduce cheating and test anxiety. As Stephens (2004) notes, if we want to increase academic integrity then "learning should be integrally connected with each assessment so that students understand how it meaningfully represents what they should be learning" (p. 3).

To help students understand the connection of every assignment to the learning outcomes (or learning objectives) of the course, a description of each outcome should be included in the syllabus (or in a supplemental handout) along with explicit directions and a rubric for the assignment. A rubric "explains to students the criteria against which their work will be judged . . . [and] makes public key criteria that students can use in developing, revising, and judging their own work" (Huba & Freed, 2000, p. 155). Rubrics are especially helpful for at-risk and unprepared students because "rubrics divide an assignment into its component parts and provide a detailed description of what constitutes acceptable or unacceptable levels of performance for each of those parts" (Stevens & Levi, 2005, p. 3).

Rubrics also help prevent cheating (especially plagiarism and fabrication) from any student in your class. A well-designed rubric, which should be given to students before they begin the assignment (e.g., research paper, project, portfolio, oral presentation), can provide direction and assistance in preparing and completing the assignment. With this kind of support, students are less likely to suddenly come up with a product that is plagiarized or fabricated. Without this kind of support, some students will resort to ordering an online term paper the day before it is due, especially if the assignment is very general and without subtopics directly related to a specific course.

Individual Feedback

Rubrics can save grading time for professors, but they also can be used to convey effective feedback and promote student learning (Stevens & Levi, 2005).[1] Using a rubric to give students specific individual feedback is

---

[1] For step-by-step assistance with developing rubrics, I highly recommend two books: *Introduction to Rubrics* by Stevens and Levi (2005) and *Learner-Centered Assessment on College Campuses* by Huba and Freed (2000).

extremely valuable for at-risk students, especially when used for first or second drafts of a project or paper. For example, hand out a rubric before students write and turn in their first drafts. Then, when students turn in their first draft, use the rubric to give students detailed feedback on how they can improve their paper for the final draft. I require students to turn in the first draft and the rubric that was scored with the revised final version. Students are told that revisions will not be graded without these items. If improvements are not made, the first draft score remains the same. For at-risk students, this process rescues them from a poor grade, which many would otherwise receive without the revision process. For an undergraduate course, I allow at least one more revision after the final paper is due. Thus, students have the option of using the feedback on the rubric to correct and/ or revise their paper one more time. (Again, revised papers will not be accepted without the first and second paper and scored rubrics.)

The process of giving individual feedback and then allowing students to make improvements will provide the opportunity for ongoing assessment directly connected to the courses' learning outcomes. This process promotes academic integrity and facilitates students' understanding of what they are learning.

Plagiarism Tutorials

In addition to using rubrics to reduce chances of plagiarism, I recommend two additional class activities. First, take some class time to discuss plagiarism. Go over plagiarism definitions, why it is important to know what plagiarism is, and how to avoid plagiarism. Some students will plagiarize by accident, carelessness, or not understanding the rules of proper citation or acceptable paraphrasing. By going over these things in class, we can let students know that such excuses are not acceptable.

A second class activity for reducing chances of plagiarism is to have students complete plagiarism tutorials. Many college libraries have developed a resource Web page specifically about plagiarism.[2] Some of them also have tutorials that let students practice recognizing and understanding plagiarism.

---

[2] One example is http://www.library.arizona.edu/help/tutorials/plagiarism/index.html

The Plagiarism Court: You Be the Judge (Islam, 2007) is an excellent tutorial that has lessons about plagiarism, consequences of plagiarism, other information on documentation, note-taking tips for avoiding copying errors, paraphrasing points, and finally a quiz. This site also has an online 11-minute video about plagiarism and inappropriate collaboration called *The Dr. Dhil Show*, directed by Jared Mezzocchi, which is humorous and informative. Students can complete this tutorial on their own, or it can be adapted to be used as a class activity.

Stanford University also provides an excellent tutorial module, *Plagiarism? It's Your Call* (2008). Original passages are posted along with examples of how the passages are paraphrased and cited. Students are asked to decide whether the paraphrased samples are correct. When using this Web page, I have students discuss their answers in small groups. Then together we look at the feedback on the Web page. This site also includes a definition and examples of plagiarism, the university's honor code, tips for avoiding plagiarism, citation rules, and so on.

Universal Design for Instruction

In addition to providing students with activities for learning about plagiarism, we need to provide unprepared college students with additional resources. We can help prevent students from taking academic shortcuts by giving them resources on how to help themselves. For ideas on how to do this effectively, consider some of the specific principles developed by Scott, McGuire, and Embry (2002) for implementing the Universal Design Instruction (UDI) model:

> [UDI] is an approach to teaching that consists of the proactive design and use of inclusive instructional strategies that benefit a broad range of learners including students with disabilities. . . . UDI operates on the premise that the planning and delivery of instruction as well as the evaluation of learning can incorporate inclusive attributes that embrace diversity in learners without compromising academic standards. (p. 1)

UDI can be very beneficial in building student rapport, providing fair access to all material for all students, providing resources for additional help, and showing students that we care about their progress. UDI principles provide a framework for inclusive and effective college instruction so that students with learning or other disabilities and unprepared students have a greater chance of success.

One of the principles, referred to as *equitable use*, suggests that faculty provide instructions that are "designed to be useful to and accessible by people with diverse abilities" (Scott, Shaw, & McGuire, in press, p. 2). To implement this principle, Scott et al. suggest that professors use "web-based courseware products with links to on-line supports and resources so all students can access materials as needed regardless of varying academic preparation, or need for review of content" (p. 2). Earlier in this book, I recommend having review sessions during office hours or inviting students who perform poorly to come to your office for extra help. Using online supports and additional resources can also help unprepared students fill in the gaps.

Another principle of UDI is *tolerance for error*, which is defined as having instruction that "anticipates variation in individual student learning pace and prerequisite skills" (Scott et al., in press, p. 3). An example of how to implement this principle is to structure long-term course projects so that "students have the option of turning in individual project components separately for constructive feedback and for integration into the final product" (p. 3). This particular example can be enhanced with the use of rubrics. Stephens (2004) recommends that we provide formative feedback for all assessments that we use in our class as a part of good teaching. Furthermore, by giving students feedback on the components of a long-term project, we can guide them as they progress. Students will also become invested in their project, and when that happens, the likelihood of them cheating is very small.

A Vocabulary Strategy for Improving Comprehension

In McCabe and Pavela's (2003) *Ten Principles of Academic Integrity*, one principle is to "foster a love of learning" (p. 1). This principle means that "academic integrity is reinforced by high academic standards. Most students will thrive in an atmosphere where academic work is seen as challenging, relevant, useful, and fair" (p. 1). However, if the academic work is too challenging and beyond what a person can do, then the student might miss the point of its relevancy and usefulness. Often reading assignments are too difficult for at-risk and unprepared students to comprehend.

Bean (2001) notes that an "inadequate vocabulary hampers the reading comprehension of many students" (p. 136) and he recommends that professors assist them with unfamiliar vocabulary, especially technical terms or words used in unusual ways, to help students become better readers (p. 148). Students with poor vocabularies are often frustrated in reading and comprehending college textbooks because ". . . the meaning of every tenth word is unknown" (Gabriel, 1999b, p. 3). Students with learning disabilities who have access to books on tape or computer programs that "read" the material to them will still have poor comprehension if their word knowledge is inadequate.

Vocabulary deficiencies can also impede a student's ability to take in information in a class setting. While many college professors are eloquent in their use of academically sophisticated terminology, many unprepared students listen to their lectures with an inadequate and limited vocabulary. More than one at-risk freshman has told me, "I can't even understand what the professor is saying. He uses words I have never heard of."

If students cannot understand the readings or lectures, they may feel a sense of desperation and lack of hope as exams approach, and the temptation to get inappropriate assistance (or simply cheat) in order to pass can be great. To prevent this kind of situation, students must improve their reading and listening comprehension by expanding their vocabulary level. To address vocabulary deficiencies, students can use the dictionary. However, after finding a definition, most students will quickly forget it a few hours later. At-risk students need a strategy for building and retaining a college-level vocabulary.

For over 20 years, I have taught at-risk students a vocabulary strategy that has proven to be effective. This strategy (complete with lessons and practice tests) is described in the teacher's manual *Learn the Lingo: A Strategy for Building a Better Vocabulary* (Gabriel, 1999b). This strategy can be taught to individuals during office hours, small groups at review or tutoring sessions, or in class. The five steps are described in greater detail in Appendix D. Briefly, students begin by writing the new word or phrase on the front of a 3-x-5-inch card. All other information goes on the reverse side of the card: (a) the chapter and page number where the word appears in the text, (b) its part of speech, (c) the word's pronunciation guide, (d) the definition, and (e) an illustration. The illustration is the most important step of this strategy. Students are told to think of an image that connects or links the definition to the word for them, and then draw a picture representing that image on the back of the card. I remind students to think about what they already know (their prior experience or knowledge) and connect the new information with it. (Some texts have helpful illustrations.) Cutting and pasting pictures from another source does not have the same kind of impact. The drawing must be personal and hand drawn by the student, regardless of drawing skills.

Figure 8.2 illustrates two vocabulary cards made by two at-risk students. Making the cards takes time, but the process can have a tremendous impact on improving the students' vocabulary skills and gives them an effective method for learning and remembering words they encounter throughout their college careers. Former at-risk students often tell me that this strategy was one of the most helpful and useful methods they used throughout college (Gabriel, 2005, p. 111).

When teaching this strategy, you should remind students that even though they will probably not be asked to define vocabulary words on course exams, making the cards will improve their reading of college texts and their listening comprehension of lectures. Once the cards are made, students can self-test using the cards. As students master the words, the cards can easily be separated into two stacks: one for words mastered and a second stack for words not yet learned.

This strategy incorporates several types of learning styles and uses principles from the science of learning. Students re-represent the information in an alternative format (visual and pictorial) as they make the cards, they connect new information to their prior knowledge, and they practice retrieval using their cards. All of these actions promote long-term retention and transfer of the new information (see chapter 5 for further discussion).

FIGURE 8.2
Vocabulary Card Samples

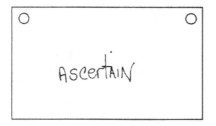

These examples show both sides of the 3-x-5-inch card that students made. Their pictures go with the new vocabulary word. The students' pictures reflect their own prior knowledge and experience, which also personalizes the new word.

There are other learning strategies for reading, writing, note taking, and preparing for tests that most professors do not have time to teach students. I like sharing the vocabulary strategy since it takes very little time to teach; students have immediate success using it; and learning this strategy helps many realize that if this one thing helps them with their reading, there are additional methods for improving other academic skills they can also acquire. I then refer students to the campus tutoring centers, writing centers, online resources, and so on.

By teaching the vocabulary strategy to at-risk students who need help with their reading comprehension, we can demonstrate to students that we care about their learning. "Students cheat more when they see the teacher as less fair and caring and when their motivation in the course is more focused on grades and less on learning and understanding" (Stephens, 2004, p. 2).

As the at-risk students learn how to learn, they will experience growth in their vocabulary skills, reading comprehension skills, writing skills, note-taking skills, and test preparation skills. As students "master cognitive skills, they develop a growing sense of their intellectual efficacy" (Bandura, 1994, p. 11). As caring teachers, the assistance we give to students can provide a framework for cultivating a strong sense of cognitive self-efficacy. By teaching (or advising) students how to prepare for tests, incidents of cheating will be reduced.

Prevention Techniques for Tests

When administering tests, there are several steps that we must take to reduce the chances of academic dishonesty and to create an atmosphere of fairness to all. When students think that other students are getting away with cheating or that a teacher will not take measures to make sure that students do not cheat, many will feel that they have to cheat to level the playing field (McCabe & Trevino, 1996). By implementing the following three steps, which are included in McCabe and Pavela's (2003) *Principles of Academic Integrity*, we can communicate to all our students that we will not tolerate academic dishonesty:

1. Affirm the importance of academic integrity;
2. Reduce opportunities to engage in academic dishonesty;
3. Develop fair and relevant tests (and/or forms of assessment). (p. 1)

To implement the first step, professors must affirm, with our students, the importance of academic integrity and honesty. To do this, we should have a statement on our syllabi along with a reference to the college's academic integrity policy (or at least list the Web site where the policy can be found). In addition, we need to talk to our students about academic integrity and what it means. We need to give examples of what we consider to be cheating and what types of collaboration will be allowed (or not allowed) on different assignments. It is also helpful to give students suggestions on how to study for exams and to post information on tutoring on campus.

We can also go over our university procedures and due process steps for anyone accused of cheating. Students should know that the procedures are in place to protect students from false or unfair accusations. McCabe and Pavela (2003) suggest that we remind our students that "institutions of higher education are dedicated to the pursuit of truth. Faculty members need to affirm that the pursuit of truth is grounded in certain core values, including diligence, civility, and honesty" (p. 1).

A second step in preventing cheating is to reduce opportunities for students to engage in academic dishonesty by establishing ground rules for taking tests. Inform students what they can bring to class (calculator, pen, or pencil) and what they cannot bring to class (backpack, earphones, or cell phone). Consider implementing the following suggestions when administering exams:

1. Know your students' names and faces; if that is not possible (i.e., large class) require students to show their identification cards (Davis, 1993, p. 307; Wankat, 2002, p. 129).

2. Do not allow students to wear baseball hats or hats that hide wandering eyes.

3. Have students spread out; if the classroom is too small for this, try to reserve a larger classroom for test day. If that is not possible, use random seat assignments so that friends cannot sit together (Davis, 1993, p. 307; McKeachie, 1994, p. 99).

4. Have at least two versions of the exam for larger classes (Davis, 1993, p. 306; McKeachie, 2002, p. 99).

5. Be present on test day (Davis, 1993, p. 306; Wankat, 2002, p. 129).

6. Warn students ahead of time if you will not permit bathroom privileges so they can be prepared.

7. Ensure that classroom management is in place so that the room is quiet (McKeachie, 1994, p. 84).

8. Explain or remind students of all the testing procedures and rules (Wankat, 2002, p. 86).

By implementing the above testing procedures, the opportunities to engage in academic dishonesty are dramatically reduced.

A third step we can take to prevent cheating is to develop fair and relevant tests. In classes where exams are part of the grade, we should write new tests every semester. Wankat (2002) suggests that we keep an "idea" file for test questions (p. 84) and after writing a test, solve it (even the essay questions) before finalizing it. "By solving the test first, you will find questions that are ambiguous, cannot be solved, are too long or too hard, or are trivial" (p. 84). Wankat also reminds us to time ourselves when we take the test:

> The time it takes you to solve the test can be used to estimate the time it will take students to solve the test. As a rule of thumb, try multiplying your solution time by five for first year students, four for juniors, and three for graduate students. Adjust these factors until you obtain good predictions. (p. 84)

Following these guidelines will help us develop fair tests for our students. "Professors who develop good rapport with students and give tests that the students think are fair will have only a small amount of cheating in their classes" (Wankat, 2002, p. 87).

Know University Standards

After high school graduation, I was able to start college but only as a special-admit freshman. I received a notice to see the dean in the administration building. I do not remember the man's exact title, but I do remember his warning: "If you do not pass your classes with at least a 2.0 cumulative grade point average by the end of the year, you will not be allowed to continue at the college." He also told me to take only 12 unit hours each semester for the first year, and keep all extracurricular activities to a minimum. Special-admit students were not allowed to join a sorority or fraternity or participate in student government. His speech scared me but also heightened my awareness of the importance of grades at the college level. Even though I do not think I knew exactly what a "cumulative" GPA was, or the exact policies concerning academic probation and dismissal, I knew that I needed to be serious.

That was many years ago, but even in this day and age, most freshmen are not aware of or do not clearly understand their university's academic standards. Policies regarding academic probation and dismissal are in the college catalog but may not be mentioned at college orientations or initial advising sessions. For at-risk and unprepared students who traditionally have not had much success making it to graduation, they should have a clear understanding of these policies and what to do if they are placed on academic probation, or dismissed.

Every academic year, despite our efforts to assist at-risk students, someone will earn an F and come to our office in tears and with a sad story that the F in our class means that the student will be academically dismissed from the college. Just as we want students to understand how they are graded and evaluated in our course, it is important for them to understand the academic standards of the university. Before responding to the student, we can refer them to their academic adviser, who will help them understand the college's probation and academic dismissal rules, or if we have the information, we can explain to the student that no one is dismissed in one semester by one grade. We should also redirect the student's attention to the course syllabus, the resources that have been provided, and the resources that we listed. By having a fair and clear grading system, no student should be surprised by his or her final grade at the end of the semester, or the consequences of receiving such a grade.

Conclusion

To guard against academic dishonesty, learner-centered teaching is our best defense. "Students consistently indicate that when they feel part of a campus community, when they believe faculty are committed to their courses, and when they are aware of the policies of their institution concerning academic integrity, they are less likely to cheat" (McCabe & Trevino, 1996, p. 34). We can promote honesty and integrity with our students by using a criterion-referenced grading system, providing a variety of ways for students to demonstrate what they are learning, using rubrics to provide individualized corrective and positive feedback, applying principles based on Universal Instruction Design, introducing learning strategies to those who are unprepared, and implementing prevention techniques.

FINAL THOUGHTS

Promoting a Richer Campus Environment

I always remember an epitaph, which is in the cemetery at Tombstone, Arizona. It says: "Here lies Jack Williams. He done his damnedest." I think that is the greatest epitaph a man can have—when he gives everything that is in him to do the job he has before him. That is all you can ask of him and that is what I have tried to do.

—Harry S. Truman

Throughout this book, I have attempted to convey the idea that as educators, it is imperative that we involve at-risk and unprepared students in the educational process and engage them in meaningful educational activities to enable them to maximize their abilities. In addition to increased engagement in classes, providing these students with various types of support and follow-up, high expectations, and corrective feedback will help them to make major improvements that will allow them to succeed in college.

As professors we are not alone in our efforts to support at-risk and unprepared students. Support for our students is also available from academic advisers, librarians, and retention specialists. In addition, counselors and tutors are available at specialized support centers on campus—tutoring centers, math and writing labs, multicultural centers, student-athlete academic centers, and the disabled student services center. We need to create two-way streets and communicate with the centers we wish our students to use. In so doing, these centers' effectiveness will also improve. Communication, networking, and teamwork across college campuses will only benefit the students and the faculty.

Many colleges and universities also have teaching centers, often called the Center for Teaching and Learning Excellence or something similar. The staff at these teaching centers can provide further help implementing the teaching methods presented in this book along with additional learner-centered teaching techniques and supporting materials. Most teaching centers also have Web sites, workshops, and other types of services for their teaching faculty and graduate assistants. I urge readers to seek out their assistance and support.

Many professors and support personnel have told me that while they are willing to reach out to at-risk and unprepared students, these students rarely seek help from them. However, by using many of the methods described in this book, I have found that at-risk and unprepared students will respond in a positive way and will use the help that is offered and benefit from it. Astin (1999) points out that "underprepared students have historically been the ones most likely to drop out at any level of education" (p. 13). But, as professors, we can make a difference in helping at-risk and unprepared students stay in college; become successful; graduate; and, at the same time, become prepared for lifelong learning.

Finally, on a personal note, I have worked with numerous professors who expanded their pedagogy to include learner-centered teaching techniques. These faculty members have told me that in using these techniques, they also developed a new and revived exuberance for teaching. At the end of the day, effective teachers need to have a genuine enthusiasm for teaching and a sincere interest in *all* of our students' learning. The techniques and strategies set forth in this book can assist all of us in advancing our passion for teaching and learning.

CHECKLIST FOR POSSIBLE COURSE SYLLABI ITEMS

A well-designed syllabus benefits both teacher and students by explicitly describing the criteria for success in the class. Items that are appropriate to include in a syllabus are listed below; however, not all items will apply to every class. This checklist can be used as a guide as you write a syllabus for a particular class.

ITEM		Notes/Comments
Instructor (and Teaching Assistant) Information		
Name		
Office location(s)		
Office phone number(s)		
E-mail		
Office hours		
Appointments or drop-ins		
Teaching philosophy		
Course Information		
Title of course		
Semester course is being offered		
Day, time, room number		
Credits (or unit hours)		
Prerequisites or corequisites		
Use of blackboard/Web CT Web Site		
Welcome message from instructor		
Course format, that is, learner centered; active learning and participation		

ITEM		Notes/Comments
Course Description		
Formal (could be the catalog description)		
Course goals		
Intended Learning Outcomes (Preferred format is a bulleted list)		
Motivational information		
Tips on succeeding in the course		
Outline of topics (or course calendar)		
Other?		
Materials		
Titles and authors of required/recommended books		
Titles, authors, and locations of books on reserve		
Cost and location of the publishing packet		
Calculators/disks, CDs, student response systems		
Lab supplies/art supplies		
Classroom Policies		
Attendance and tardiness		**Reminder:** All ground rules should adhere to the following criteria: (a) definable, (b) reasonable, (c) enforceable. (An unenforced or unenforceable rule is worse than no rule at all.)
Participation in discussions or activities		
Civility/code of conduct (check university Web site)		
Cell phones, beepers, and pagers		
Newspapers and food		
Academic integrity (check university Web site)		
Class notes/handouts availability		
Seating options (i.e., seating chart, or ???)		

ITEM		Notes/Comments
Assignments, Assessment, and Evaluation		
Grading criteria, weight of assignments and exams		
Kinds of papers or projects		
Due dates, submission procedures		
Kinds of exams, dates		
Reading assignments, due dates		
Acceptability of handwritten work		
Typing styles requirement (including American Psychological Association, Modern Language Association, other style requirements)		
Rewrite and makeup policies		
Policy on late assignments		
Testing procedures or policies		
Code of academic integrity statement		
Student Support Services		
Disability services/accommodation policies		
Writing center support		
Learning resources center (or support)		
Counseling/consultation		
Department or college resources/Web page		
Instructional Approach/Emphasis		
Writing intensive		
Service learning, practicum, internship		
Case studies		
Cooperative learning activities		
Team-based learning (i.e., Michaelsen, Knight, & Fink, 2002)		
Peer reviews, or sharing		

ITEM		Notes/Comments
Health, Safety, or Ethical Requirements		
Lab procedures		
Ethical conduct for use of human subjects		
Confidentiality requirement		
Other Useful Information		
Study time expected		
Withdrawal dates		
College/departmental requirements		
Team member contact info (or study buddies info)		
Subject to change notice		

From "Starting the Semester on the Right Foot: 40 Concrete Ideas to Take Into the Classroom Tomorrow," by N. Bellows, 2003. *Teaching and Learning News, 13*(1), p. 6.

Note. Original version of this checklist came from Maureen Zimmerman, Mesa CC. Modified by and updated by Susan Ledlow, George Watson, Laura Bush, and Veronica Patoja from Arizona State University. Further modified by Randi Lydum and Kathleen Gabriel from University of Arizona. Used by permission.

PERFORMANCE PROGNOSIS INVENTORY FOR
ANALYTICAL CHEMISTRY

By
Dr. Saundra Y. McGuire
Director, Center for Academic Success
Adj. Professor Department of Chemistry
B-31 Coates Hall
Louisiana State University
Baton Rouge, LA 70803

The inventory below lists behaviors that you should exhibit in order to excel in analytical chemistry. Write true or false beside each of the following statements describing the way you will study in this class. The scoring scale is on the reverse side.

1. I will always read the lecture material before I go to lecture.
2. I will go over my lecture notes as soon as possible after lecture to rework them and mark problem areas.
3. I will learn the relevant concepts from General Chemistry so that I have the background necessary to understand the material in Analytical Chemistry.
4. I will try to work the homework problems without looking at the example problems or my notes from class.
5. I will go to office hours or tutoring regularly to discuss problems on the homework.
6. I will rework all of the homework problems before the test or quiz.
7. I will spend some time studying analytical chemistry at least five days per week (outside of class time).
8. I will "teach" the concepts to friends, myself in the mirror, stuffed animals, imaginary students, etc.

9. I will make flashcards and use mnemonics for myself to help me remember facts and equations.

10. I will make diagrams or draw mental pictures of the concepts, experimental procedures and instruments discussed in class.

11. I will actively participate in my study group where we will discuss homework problems and quiz ourselves on the material.

12. I will rework all of the quiz and test items I have missed before the next class session.

13. I know that I can make an A in this class, and will put forth the effort to do so.

(scoring on the reverse side)

Reverse Side

The predicted grade for your performance this semester is provided below:

Number of True Responses	Predicted Grade
10–13	A
6–9	B
4–5	C
2–3	D
less than 2	F

Note that you can change your predicted grade at any point by changing your behavior such that more of the statements are true.

PREPARING FOR THREE DIFFERENT GROUPINGS

Sample Groupings for a Class of 33 Students

NUMBER	COLOR	TIME	STUDENT'S NAME
5	BLUE	10 AM	
1	GREEN	10 AM	
4	ORANGE	10 AM	
7	YELLOW	10 AM	
2	BLACK	12 NOON	
4	BROWN	12 NOON	
3	RED	12 NOON	
7	VIOLET	12 NOON	
8	BLACK	3 PM	
6	BLUE	3 PM	
9	PINK	3 PM	
6	BROWN	4 PM	
2	GREEN	4 PM	
3	PINK	4 PM	
4	YELLOW	4 PM	
1	RED	5 AM	
3	GREEN	5 PM	
8	PINK	5 PM	
5	YELLOW	5 PM	
1	PURPLE	6 AM	
9	TURQUOISE	6 AM	
8	VIOLET	6 AM	
9	BROWN	7 PM	
6	ORANGE	7 PM	
2	RED	7 PM	

NUMBER	COLOR	TIME	STUDENT'S NAME
1	BLUE	8 AM	
5	ORANGE	8 AM	
3	PURPLE	8 AM	
6	TURQUOISE	8 AM	
4	BLACK	9 AM	
7	PURPLE	9 AM	
5	TURQUOISE	9 AM	
2	VIOLET	9 AM	

Grouping Strategy: Divide your class into three groups using numbers, colors, and time of day. To do this, first adjust the list above to fit the size of your class. If you want each group size to be 3 students, or if you have more or fewer than 33 students, add or subtract from the list. In the "table" menu, you can use the "sort" tool key to rearrange the chart by categories. (For example, you can sort the color column so that all the colors—that is, all reds, all pinks, all yellows, and so on—are together.)

Once you have adjusted the list for a specific class, make up a 3-x-5-inch card for each line on your adjusted list (see sample card on next page). Then, before class, shuffle the cards. As students come into class, have the students draw one of the cards or after they have taken a seat, go around the room and give each student a card.

After the cards are distributed, each student will write his or her name on the card and give it back to you. From the random card drawing, you can create a master list for each grouping. Then when students form a group, you can tell them whether they are to get into their number group, color group, or time of day group. By having three group possibilities, students will have the opportunity to meet and work with lots of other students in the class.

SAMPLE CARD

#1

RED

5 AM

Name_____

VOCABULARY STRATEGY STEPS

Instructions for Students

The steps described below are from Gabriel's (1999a) *Learn the Lingo: A Strategy for Building a Better Vocabulary, Student Booklet, Volume I.* Teacher's manuals (Vol. 1 and Vol. 2) with 10 lessons and quizzes for each are available from kgabriel@u.arizona.edu. (Volume 2 of the student booklet is also available. Send requests to kgabriel@u.arizona.edu.)

STEP 1

Write the vocabulary word (or key word printed in bold from your textbook) in the center of a 3 x 5 card that has holes punched at the top. The punched holes should be the same width as binder rings so the card can easily be clipped into your binder (see Fig. 1). You should write the word neatly and in a "normal" size print or cursive. (Large block print should not be used.)

FIGURE 1
The front of a Vocabulary Card should have only the vocabulary word written on it. No other information should appear on the front.

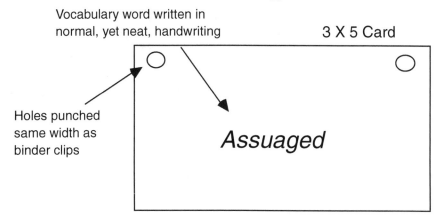

Use your normal handwriting because that will assist in the brain-hand linkage and in memory retention. *Example*: assuaged (from the first page of the novel *To Kill a Mockingbird*).

STEP 2

Flip the card over so that the holes are now on the bottom. For a new vocabulary word, write the word's part of speech in the upper right-hand corner of the card (see Fig. 2). For a word from a textbook, write the chapter number and/or page number where the key word or bold printed word is.

STEP 3

If needed, write the word's pronunciation guide in the upper left-hand corner of the card. This step is optional (see Fig. 2).

STEP 4

Write the word's definition on the bottom of the card, leaving the middle part empty. Look up unknown words and break down the definition until it makes sense. If you are using a textbook, avoid using the textbook's glossary. Instead read through the paragraph that the word is embedded in.

STEP 5

This is the most important step in making the card. Think of an "image" that connects or links the definition to the word and then draw a "picture"

FIGURE 2

Information is written at the top and bottom of the card so that there is room in the middle for your drawing.

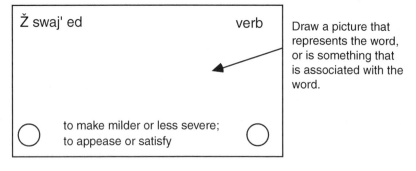

representing that image. Think about your prior experience (or knowledge) and connect the new information to what you already know. Figure out what image best fits for you. Some texts will have illustrations that will be helpful. The picture should be drawn in the center of the card.

At first, the drawings may be awkward; however, it is extremely important not to have just a visual image connection, but also to be consistent with this connection, and therefore the picture is needed. You don't have to be an artist—a simple figure will do. Try working with fellow students (or a tutor) if you get stuck. Figure 3 gives some examples to illustrate how pictures from different students can be very different for the same word because their personal experience and prior knowledge are different.

Self-Test Using Your Vocabulary Cards

After you have made your own vocabulary cards, there are different ways to self-test. One way is to lay out all the cards with the word on the front, face

FIGURE 3
These are examples of different drawings for the same word. In the drawing at the top, the student has drawn a person being sworn in *before* testifying in court; in the drawing at the bottom, the student has drawn the coin toss, which happens *before* a football game starts.

up. Then, pick out one card and say the definition without looking on the back. After you say the answer to yourself, you need to look at the answer on the back of the card. If your answer is correct, pick up the card. If it is wrong, the card stays on the table. This process is repeated until all the cards are picked up. Once all the cards are up, you should lay the cards out again and repeat the self-test.

When self-testing, if there is a word that you are not sure of, you can "peek" at the picture to see if it triggers your memory. Since the definition is at the bottom of the card, only turn the card half over, so it cannot be seen. If the picture does not help, then the picture needs to be fixed or changed. Any card "peeked at" stays on the table until the prompt is not needed. Self-testing should take place for several days after the cards are made, and before the actual test is to be given.

REFERENCES

Adelman, C. (2004). *Principal indicators of student academic histories in postsecondary education, 1972–2000: U.S. Department of Education.* Washington, DC: Institute of Education Sciences.

Angelo, T. A., & Cross, K. P. (1993). *Classroom assessment techniques* (2nd ed.). San Francisco: Jossey-Bass.

Astin, A. (1999). Rethinking academic "excellence." *Liberal Education, 85*(2), 8–19.

Baecker, D. (1998). Uncovering the rhetoric of the syllabus. *College Teaching, 46*(2), 58–62.

Bandura, A. (1994). Self-efficacy. In V. S. Ramachaudran (Ed.), *Encyclopedia of human behavior* (Vol. 4, pp. 71–81). New York: Academic Press. Retrieved from http://www.des.emory.edu/mfp/Bandura1994EHB.pdf (15 pages).

Barr, R., & Tagg, J. (1995). From teaching to learning—A new paradigm for undergraduate education. *Change, 27*(6), 12–26.

Bean, J. (2001). *Engaging ideas: The professor's guide to integrating writing, critical thinking and active learning in the classroom.* San Francisco: Jossey-Bass.

Bellows, N. (2003). Starting the semester on the right foot: 40 concrete ideas to take into the classroom tomorrow. *Teaching and Learning News, 13*(1), pp. 6–7. Center for Teaching Excellence, University of Maryland, College Park. http://www.cte.umd.edu/teaching/newsletter/2003-04/SepOct03.pdf

Biggs, J., Kember D., & Leung D. (2001). The revised two-factor study process questionnaire: R-spq-2f. *British Journal of Educational Psychology, 71*, 133–149.

Blose, G. (1999). Modeled retention and graduation rates: Calculating expected retention and graduation rates for multicampus university systems. *New Directions for Higher Education, 27*(4), 69–86.

Bourner, T. (1997). Teaching methods for learning outcomes. *Education + Training, 39*(9), 344–348.

Bransford, J., Brown, A., & Cocking, R. (Eds.). (2000). *How people learn: Brain, mind, experience, and school.* Washington, DC: National Academy Press.

Brocato, J. (1989). How much does coming to class matter? Some evidence of class attendance and grade performance. *Educational Research Quarterly, 13*, 3–6.

Chickering, A., & Gamson, Z. (1987). Seven principles for good practice in under-graduate education. *Washington Center News*. Retrieved from http://learning commons.evergreen.edu/pdf/fall1987.pdf

Chung, C., & Hsu, L. (2006). Encouraging students to seek help: Supplementing office hours with a course center. *College Teaching, 54*(3), 253–258.

Davis, B. (1993). *Tools for teaching*. San Francisco: Jossey-Bass.

Desrochers, C. (1999). Multi-purpose lecture breaks. *The Teaching Professor, 13*(10), 1–2.

Felder, R., & Brent, R. (1996). Navigating the bumpy road to student-centered instruction. *College Teaching, 44*, 43–47. Retrieved from http://www4.ncsu.edu/unity/lockers/users/f/felder/public/Papers/Resist.html

Felder, R., & Solomon, B. (n.d.) *Learning styles and strategies*. North Carolina State University, Raleigh. Retrieved from http://www4.ncsu.edu/unity/lockers/users/f/felder/public/ILSdir/styles.htm

Felder, R., & Soloman, B. (1991). *Index of learning styles questionnaire*. North Carolina State University, Raleigh. Retrieved from http://www.engr.ncsu.edu/learningstyles/ilsweb.html

Fleming, N. (2001–2006). *VARK: A guide to learning styles*. Retrieved from http://www.vark-learn.com/english/index.asp

Friedman, P., Rodriguez, F., & McComb, J. (2001). Why students do and do not attend classes: Myths and realities. *College Teaching, 49*(4), 124–134.

Gabriel, K. (1999a). *Learn the lingo: A strategy for building a better vocabulary. Student booklet (Vol. 1)*. Tucson, Arizona: KFG Educational Consultants.

Gabriel, K. (1999b). *Learn the lingo: A strategy for building a better vocabulary. Teacher's manual (Vol. 1)*. Tucson, Arizona: KFG Educational Consultants.

Gabriel, K. (2005). *Starting behind . . . finishing ahead: A blueprint for academic support for at-risk college students*. Tucson, Arizona: KFG Educational Consultants.

Grunert, J. (1997). *The course syllabus: A learning-centered approach*. Bolton, MA: Anker.

Halawah, I. (2006). The impact of student-faculty informal interpersonal relationships on intellectual and personal development. *College Student Journal, 40*(3), 670–678.

Halpern, D., & Hakel, M. (2003, July/August). Applying the science of learning to the university and beyond: Teaching for long-term retention and transfer. *Change, 35*, 36–41.

Hassel, H., & Lourey, J. (2005). The dea(r)th of student responsibility. *College Teaching, 53*(1), 2–13.

Herteis, E. (2003). Creating a culture of academic integrity at the U of S. *Bridges, 1*(3), 1.

Hester, E. (1998). Taking meta-cognitive moments. *The Teaching Professor, 12*(2), 2.

Horn, L., & Berger, R. (2004). *College persistence on the rise? Changes in 5-Year degree completion and postsecondary persistence rates between 1994 and 2000* (NCES 2005-156). U.S. Department of Education, National Center for Education Statistics. Washington, DC: U.S. Government Printing Office.

Huba, M. E., & Freed, J. E. (2000). *Learner-centered assessment on college campuses: Shifting the focus from teaching to learning.* Boston: Allyn & Bacon.

Islam, R. (2007). *The plagiarism court: You be the judge.* Retrieved from http://www.fairfield.edu/x13870.html

Jaasma, M. A., & Koper, R. J. (1999). The relationship of student-faculty out-of-class communication to instructor immediacy and trust and to student motivation. *Communication Education, 48*, 41–47.

Kiewra, K., & Dubois, N. (1998). *Learning to learn: Making the transition from student to life-long learner.* Boston: Allyn & Bacon.

Kuh, G., Kinzie, J., Buckley, J., Bridges, B., & Hayek, J. (2006, July). *What matters to student success: A review of the literature.* Retrieved from http://nces.ed.gov/npec/pdf/Kuh_Team_Report.pdf

Kuh, G., Kinzie, J., Cruce, T., Shoup, R., & Gonyea, R. (2007, January). Connecting the dots: Multi-faceted analyses of the relationships between student engagement results from the NSSE, and the institutional practices and conditions that foster student success. Retrieved from http://nsse.iub.edu/pdf/Connecting_the_Dots_Report.pdf

Kuh, G., Kinzie, J., Schuh, J., Whitt, E., & Associates. (2005). *Student success in college: Creating conditions that matter.* San Francisco: Jossey-Bass.

Ledlow, S. (2005, August). Fall Workshop for Tri-University Grant on Learner-Centered Education, Flagstaff, Arizona.

Light, R. (2001). *Making the most of college: Students speak their minds.* Cambridge, MA: Harvard University Press.

Maxwell, J. (2007). *Talent is never enough.* Nashville, TN: Nelson Business.

McBrayer, D. (2001). Tutoring systems salvage poor performers. *The Teaching Professor, 15*(4), 3.

McCabe, D. L., & Pavela, G. (2003). *Ten principles of academic integrity*. College Administration Publications, Inc., Saint John's, Florida. Retrieved from http://www.collegepubs.com/ref/10PrinAcaInteg.shtml

McCabe, D., & Trevino, L. (1996). What we know about cheating in college. *Change, 28*(1), 28–34.

McCabe, D., & Trevino, L. (1997). Individual and contextual influences on academic dishonesty: A multi-campus investigation. *Research in Higher Education, 38*(3), 379–396.

McCabe, D., Trevino, L., & Butterfield, K. (2001). Cheating in academic institutions: A decade of research. *Ethics and Behavior, 11*(3), 219–232.

McCutcheon, L. (1989). Prediction of absenteeism in college students using social learning theory. *Community/Junior College Quarterly of Research and Practice, 13*(1), 1–10.

McKeachie, W. (2002). *Teaching tips: Strategies, research, and theory for college and university teachers* (11th ed.). Boston: Houghton Mifflin.

Mencke, R., & Hartman, S. (2000). *Learning style assessment*. http://www.ulc.arizona.edu/learning_style.php

Merrow, J. (Executive Producer), & Tulenko, J. (Senior Producer). (2005). *Declining by degrees: Higher education at risk* [videotape or DVD recording]. Produced by Learning Matters, Inc. Cleveland: Learning Matters, Public Broadcasting Service.

Michaelsen, L., Knight, A., & Fink, L. D. (2002). *Team-based learning: A transformative use of small groups in college teaching*. Sterling, VA: Stylus.

Mullens, A. (2000). Cheating to win. *University Affairs, 41*(10), 22–28.

Murphy, B. (2005). Need to get your students talking? Try speed dating! *The Teaching Professor, 19*(7), 1, 4.

Nilson, L. (1998). *Teaching at its best: A research-based resource for college instructors*. Bolton, MA: Anker.

Parkes, J., & Harris, M. (2002). The purposes of a syllabus. *College Teaching, 50*(2), 55–61.

Pascarella, E., & Terenzini, P. (2005). *How college affects students: A third decade of research* (Vol. 2). San Francisco: Jossey-Bass.

Penn, A. (Director), Coe, F. (Producer), & Gibson, W. (Writer). (1962). *The miracle worker* [Motion picture]. United States: United Artists.

Plagiarism? It's your call. (2008). Retrieved from the Stanford University Web site, http://skil.stanford.edu/module6/paraphrasing.html

Raymark, P., & Connor-Green, P. (2002). The syllabus quiz. *Teaching of Psychology, 29*(4), 286–288.

Resistance to active learning. (1995–1997). *Curricular revision starting at ground zero: The case of introductory accounting.* http://www.csuchico.edu/acms/fipse/obsta cles/resistance.html

Sanoff, A. P. (2006, March). What professors and teachers think. *The Chronicle of Higher Education.* Retrieved from http://chronicle.com/free/v52/i27/27b00901 .htm

Scott, S. S., McGuire, J. M., & Embry, P. (2002). *Universal design for instruction fact sheet.* Storrs: University of Connecticut, Center on Postsecondary Education and Disability. Retrieved from http://www.facultyware.uconn.edu/udi_factsheet.cfm

Scott, S., Shaw, S., & McGuire, J. (in press). *Universal Design for Instruction: A new paradigm for adult instruction in postsecondary education. Remedial and special education.* Retrieved from http://www.facultyware.uconn.edu/UDI_principles.htm

Sleigh, M., Ritzer, D., & Casey, M. (2002). Student versus faculty perceptions of missing class. *Teaching of Psychology, 29,* 53–56.

Stanley, C. A., & Porter, M. E. (Eds.). (2002). *Engaging large classes: Strategies and techniques for college faculty.* Bolton, MA: Anker.

Stephens, J. (2004, May). Justice or just us? What to do about cheating. *Carnegie Perspectives*: The Carnegie Foundation for the Advancement of Teaching, Stanford, CA. Retrieved from http://www.carnegiefoundation.org/perspectives/ sub.asp?key=245&subkey=577

Stevens, D., & Levi, A. (2005). *Introduction to rubrics: An assessment tool to save grading time, convey effective feedback, and promote student learning.* Sterling, VA: Stylus.

Svinicki, M. (2004). *Learning and motivation in the postsecondary classroom.* Bolton, MA: Anker.

Tyler, R. (1949, 1970). *Basic principles of curriculum and instruction.* Chicago: University of Chicago Press.

Urban, H. (2004). *Positive words, powerful results: Simple ways to honor, affirm, and celebrate life.* New York: Simon & Schuster.

Van Blerkom, M. (1992). Class attendance in undergraduate courses. *The Journal of Psychology, 126*(5), 487–495.

Wankat, P. (2002). *The effective, efficient professor: Teaching, scholarship and service.* Boston: Allyn & Bacon.

Wasley, P. (2006). Underrepresented students benefit most from 'engagement'. *The Chronicle of Higher Education, 53*(13), p. A39. Retrieved on 11/17/06 at http:// chronicle.com/weekly/v53/i13/13a03901.htm.

Watson, L., Terrell, M., Wright, D., & Associates. (2002). *How minority students experience college: Implications for planning and policy.* Sterling, VA: Stylus.

Weimer, M. (2002). *Learner-centered teaching: Five key changes to practice.* San Francisco: Jossey-Bass.

Wooden, J. (with Jamison, S.). (1997). *Wooden: A lifetime of observations and reflections on and off the court.* Chicago: Contemporary Books.

Wyatt, G. (1992, July). Skipping class: An analysis of absenteeism among first-year college students. *Teaching Sociology, 20,* 201–207.

Zull, J. (2002). *The art of changing the brain: Enriching the practice of teaching by exploring the biology of learning.* Sterling, VA: Stylus.

INDEX

absenteeism: from class, 27, 42; being absent 21, 53, 55. *See also* attendance, taking roll

academic dishonesty, 103, 104, 114,115,117

academic failure. *See* failure

academic standards, 85, 109, 110

academic support centers or programs, 3, 4, 15, 26

accountability, and students being accountable, 11, 12, 20, 22, 33, 77

active learning, 34, 53, 74, 75, 78, 121, 135, 139; resistance to, 78. *See also* class participation

activities, in class. *See* meaningful educational activities

Adelman, C., 1, 2

admission to college: special admit, 4, 10, 29, 35, 116

Angelo, T. A. & Cross, K. P., 30, 97, 98, 100, 101

anxiety: evaluation, 33, 105; test, 96, 107

assessment, 6–7, 32–33, 68–70, 75–76, 83, 85, 88–102, 107, 110, 114; on–going, 108. *See also* accountability; evaluation; grades; learning outcomes

assignments, 55, 66, 80, 114; introducing, 31, 36, 39; summative, 8; late or make-up, 20, reading, 26–27, 29, 74, 111; informal 28–29; grading of, 77, 89, 106,

Astin, A., 4, 31, 112

athletes, 16, 20, 62, 79

atmosphere, of the classroom, 5, 39, 43, 46, 50, 110, 114. *See also* climate

attendance, 6; and grades, 53–56, 64; policies of, 27; promoting and increasing, 41–44, 46, 51–52; taking roll, 43, 53–55, 96, *See also* Class Participation

Attention span, of students, 101, *See also* Interactive Lectures; Lectures

Attitudes, 1, 2, 34, 43, 51–52, 57, 65, 78, 82, 97

background knowledge, 29, 83. *See also* prior knowledge.

Baecker, D.,26, 77

Bandura, A.,79, 114

Barr, R. & Tagg, J., 74–76, 80

Bean, J., 111

behavior: avoidance, 18, ; classroom climate, 64; engaging, 5; expectations, 36, 37, 125–126; appropriate, 12, 35; problem (or inappropriate), 11, 50, 51, 81–82, 94. 103, *See also* classroom climate; ground rules

Bellows, N., 124

Biggs, J., Kember, D., & Leung, D., 67

Blose, G., 3

Bourner, T., 57

Bransford, J., Brown, A., & Cocking, R., 75–76, 82, 89

caring, 113, 114

centers, for academic support, 3, 4. *See also* programs

cheating. 7, 16, 54, 103–105, 107, 115; prevention of, 105, 107, 114–116

Chickering, A. & Gamson, Z., 6, 45, 53, 68, 70, 86

Chung, C. & Hsu, L. 5

class participation, 7, 53, 78, 85; lack of, 16; grading of, 27, 33, 39, 43, 54–55, 93, 96, 101, *See also* meaningful educational activities

classroom assessment techniques (CATs), 30, 83, 97–98, 100, 101, *See also* Angelo, T. A. and Cross, K. P.

climate, of classroom, 25, 26–28, 38, 56, 64, 69, 84, *See also* atmosphere; first day of class; first week of class commitment: from students and faculty, 13, 15–17, 25, 30, 42, 45

comprehension, 8, 88, 96, 98, 110–114

concept maps, 66, 69

connections: with new material, 7, 67, 77; with the university, 20; 28,

course syllabus, 26, 32, 39, 50, 55, 76, 121

Davis, B., 59, 64, 70, 195, 115

Declining by Degrees, 91

deep versus shallow learning, 65–67

Desrochers, C., 93

developmental studies (or courses), 2,3

diagrams, 36, 61, 68, 93, 99, 126

discussions, in class, 50, 69. *See also* class participation

disengagement: in class, 42, from college, 33

diversity, 6, 83–84, 109

due dates, 26, 38, 107, 123

educational activities. *See* meaningful educational activities

empowering students, 6, 63, 70–71, 83

encouragement: for motivation, 18; for interaction, 45, 50–51, 84, 96; for class discussion, 50; for learning, 53, 58, 64, 66, 83, 99

engagement, of students, 5, 7–8, 14, 32, 34, 42, 46, 53–54, 56, 73–74, 76, 78, 81, 91–92, 94, 97–98, 101, 114–115, 119, *See also* class participation; learner-centered education; meaningful educational activities; prior knowledge

evaluation, of students, 33, 69, 80, 105, 109, 123, *See also* assessment; grades

exams, preparing for, 57, 64, 67, 97, 111–112, 114–116; for grades, 70, 87–88

excuses, handling of, 21, 108

expectations: high levels, 3, 5, 11–12, 23, 25–26, 30, 35 58, 76–78, 83 90, 119; of behavior, 37, 38, 50, 81

expertise, of teachers, 57, 88; experienced teachers, 28, 97

extra: hours (or time), 17–18, 44, 52, 101; curricular, 18, 30, 39, 103, 116; credit, 20–21, 30; support, 41, 110

facilitate: faculty-student contact, 4, 19, 45, 52, 97; student interaction, 46, 50. *See also* group work

faculty. *See* professors.

failure, in academics, 3, 4, 14–16, 79, 104

fairness: access of material, 109; grading and tests, 21, 114–117; treatment, 111, 113

fear of failure. *See* anxiety

feedback, 7, 14, 17, 33, 37, 51, 59, 80, 88–90, 92, 96, 98, 101, 105, 107–110, 117, 119, *See also* formative assessment

Felder, R., & Brent, R., 78

Felder, R., & Solomon, B., 60–62

first day of class, 25–26, 28–29, 38–39, 45, 50, 52, 78

first week of class, 5, 20, 27–28, 43, 81. *See also* climate

Fleming, N., 62,

flexible assessment, 68, 69–70

formative assessment, 80, 89–92, 95, 97, 99, 101, 110. *See also* assessment; summative assessment

Friedman, P., Rodriguez, F., & McComb, J., 41, 53

Gabriel, K., 111–112, 124, 131

goals: course, 5–6, 25, 29, 39; student (personal), 19, 30–31, 35, 37; teaching, 30, 97; unrealistic, 33, 35, *See also* teaching goals inventory

grades: improving, 41–43, 58, 63, 73, 98, 08; measuring & assigning, 21, 32–34, 36, 55, 69–70, 77–78, 87–89, 101, 105–106, 116–117; obsession with, 7, 113; passing, 16; predicting, 36, 126; transfer, 29, *See also* assessment

ground rules, 38, 50, 64, 81, 115, 122

groups, student: work, 69; projects, 46, 50; study, 46, 100, 126; in-class, 69, 81, 96, 128

Grunert, J., 26, 30, 34, 39

Halawah, I., 4

Halpern, D., & Hakel, M., 67, 99

handouts, 75. *See also* rubrics

Hassel, H. Lourey, J., 77

Hester, E., 95, 96
high expectations. *See* expectations
Horn, L., & Berger, R., 1
Huba, M. E., & Freed, J. E., 9, 31–32, 75–76, 90, 107

ice-breaking activity, 28, 46–50
identifying at-risk students, 28–29
instructors. *See* professors
integrity and honesty, 7–8, 38, 105–110, 114, 117, 122–123, *See also* principles of academic integrity
intellectual development, 4, 50, 58, 114; commitment, 45,
interactions. *see* groups.
interactive lectures methods, 5, 43, 53, 92, 136
interventions, early, 5, 20, 31, 89
Islam, R., 109

Jaasma, M. A., & Koper, R. J., 51
journals: academic, 22–23; personal, 33
judgment-free zone, 50
Judge, You Be the, 109, *See also* plagiarism

Kiewra, K., & and Dubois, N., 98
knowledge, prior, 7, 29, 31, 66–68, 75, 82–83, 112–113
Kuh, G., Kinzie, J., Buckley, J., Bridges, B., & Hayek, J., 9–10, 50, 52, 55–56, 69–70, 80, 83–85, 90
Kuh, G., Kinzie, J., Cruce, T., Shoup, R., & Gonyea, R., 3, 31, 73
Kuh, G., Kinzie, J., Schuh, J., Whitt, E., & Associates, 1–4, 57, 73–74, 76–77, 80, 86

Learn the Lingo: A Strategy for Building a Better Vocabulary, 111, 131
learner-centered education, definition, 80
learner-centered teaching: benefits, 82, 117, 120; environment, 6, 25, 82, 85; grading, 105; syllabus, 5, 38; teaching methods, 14, 34, 69
learning outcomes, 6–7, 30–33, 39, 76–77, 90, 106–108
learning style inventories, 6, 59–60, 64
learning styles, 6, 19, 33–34, 57–58 61–70, 81, 107, 112

lectures, stand and deliver, 69, 73. *See also,* interactive lectures methods
Ledlow, S., 49, 124
library skills, 22–23
lifelong learners, 13, 120
Light, R., 31, 46, 58, 83
lighting of classroom, 64, 94
listening, 53, 75, 77, 82, 101, 111–112. *See also* attention span; comprehension

maps. *See* concept maps
matrix, for testing memory, 98–99
Maxwell, J., 21, 22
McBrayer, D., 36–37
McCabe, D., & Trevino, L., 103, 110, 114, 117
McCabe, D., Trevino, L., & Butterfield, K., 103–104
McCabe, D.L. & Pavela, 110, 114–115
McCutcheon, L., 41–42
McKeachie, W., 57, 74, 105, 115
meaningful educational activities, 43, 53, 55, 57, 76, 78–79, 85, 101, 119
memory, 44, 98–99, 132, 143. *See also* matrix; exams
Mencke, R., & Hartman, S., 61–62
Merrow, J., 91
Meta-Cognitive Moments, 95–96
Michaelsen, L., Knight, A., & Fink, L. D., 123
minority students, 3, 64, 84–85, *See also* diversity
Minute Paper, 97
Miracle Worker, The, 11
missing class or assignments, 20, 21, 27, 81, *See also* Attendance
mission, 9–10, 13, 24, 25, 30–31, 39
motivation, 5, 18, 32, 45, 51, 79, 90, 106
Mullens, A., 104
multicultural centers, 18, 119
multiple-choice, 65, 67, 91–92, 95
Murphy, B., 47

names, learning and using students', 43–46, 51, 54, 93–94, 96, 115
negative attitudes. *See* attitudes
Nilson, L., 76, 90

note-taking (class notes), 18, 26–27, 37, 62, 75, 94, 96, 101, 109, 113–114; reading notes, 64, 97

objectives (learning). *See* learning outcomes
office hours, 4, 18–19, 31, 36, 38, 44, 51, 83, 100, 110–111, 121, 125
one-minute paper, 97
online: learning style inventories, 60–62, teaching goals inventories, 30; plagiarism prevention, 109; support, 110, 113
out of class, 26, 45, 59, 60, 79
outcomes. *See* learning outcomes
overwhelmed, 22–23

Parkes, J., & Harris, M., 26, 38
participation, in class, 7, 16, 27, 33, 43, 53–55, 78, 85, 93, 101, 103
Pascarella, E., & Terenzini, P., 30, 75
peer interaction, 50, 103. *See also* groups
Penn, A., Coe. F., and Gibson, W., 11–12
philosophy of teaching, 5, 9, 10–24, 29–30
plagiarism, 107–109. *See also* cheating
point system for grading, 106. *See also* grades
policies: course, 13, 18, 26, 38–39, 122; universities, 116–117. *See also* procedures
portfolios, 33, 69, 106–107
principles of academic integrity, 110, 114
principles of good practice, 6, 45, 68, 86
Pro and Con Grid, 98, 100
problem-solving, 69, 100
procedures: course, 26, 36; test-taking, 38, 115; class activity, 97; university, 115
professors, influence on, 4, 14, 31, 41, 51, 67
programs, for academic support, 3, 4, 15, 26

questions, in class 7

Raymark, P., & Connor-Green, P., 38–39
reading: assignments, 29, 111; comprehension, 110–111; inadequate skills, 1, 15; improving, 15. *See also* comprehension
reciprocate efforts, 11, 45
reluctant students, 5, 18, 88
remedial courses, 1, 2, 4

resistance to learner-centered teaching, 34, 80; preparing for, 6, 78; countering, 78–79
respond clickers, 91, *See also* meaningful educational activities
responsibility of students, accepting of, 13, 19–20, 22, 28, 30, 58, 70–71, 76–68, 85–85, 105
rubrics, 7, 33, 106–108, 110, 117
rules. *See* climate; ground rules; policies; procedures

Sanoff, 1, 2
science of learning, 6, 67–68, 70, 99, 112
Scott, S., McGuire, J., & Embry, P., 109
Scott, S., Shaw, S., & McGuire, J., 110
self-efficacy, 79, 114
self-testing, 100, 112, 133–134, *See also* exams
Sleigh, M., Ritzer, D., & Casey, M., 41–42, 51
summative assessment, 8, 33, 89, 90, 99, 101–102, *See also* assessment; formative assessment
standards: holding high, 4, 5, 12, 70, 85, 109–110; lowering, 23, 37, 90; university, 116–117
Stanley, C.A. & Porter, M.E., 33
student–athletes. *See* athletes
Stephens, J., 107, 110
support centers. *See* tutoring centers/labs
Svinicki, M., 14, 62–63, 65, 66, 88
syllabus, 5–6, 20, 25–28, 32–35, 37–39, 45, 50–52, 55, 76–77, 107, 121–122
syllabus quiz, 39

taking roll, 43, 53–54, 96, *See also* attendance
Talent is Never Enough, 21
tardiness, 63, 81, 122
teaching assistants, 6, 56, 121
teaching goals, 5, 30, 97
teaching styles, 6, 8–9, 68
team-based learning, 76
tests. *See* exams
textbooks, using and reading, 37, 65, 111, 132
Think-Pair-Share, 93
time and commitment, 16–18, 30,

tone of course. *See* climate
tutoring centers/labs, 2–3, 15, 18–19, 34, 36–37, 41, 64–65, 88, 102, 111, 113,114, 119, 125
Tyler, R., 78
Tyus, Wyoming, 11

understanding, checking for, 87; illusion of, 88; improving, 90, 108; learning styles, 63, 69; prior knowledge, 68, 83. *See also* comprehension
Universal Design for Instruction, 109
Universal Instruction Design, 7, 109, 117
Urban, H., 19

values, 9, 45, 84–85, 97, 115
Van Blerkom, M., 53
variety: of methods, 6, 68–70, 106, 117; of activities/tasks, 33, 53; of learners, 64, 84
verbal and visuospatial learning , 61, 65, 99
visual cues or aids, 65, 69, 91, 112

visual learners, 61–62
vocabulary skills, 8, 36, 111–114, 131–133. *See also* reading comprehension

Wankat, P., 2, 26, 34, 38, 43–44, 51, 53, 58, 63, 69, 74, 101, 115–116
Wasley, P., 98
Watson, L., Terrell, M., Wright, D., & Associates. 85
Weimer, M., 1, 15, 18, 33, 58–59, 66, 74, 76, 106
Wooden, J., 22
Write-Pair-Share, 93–95
writing: skills, 3, 15, 29, 112–114; assignments, 70; labs/ centers, 3, 18, 34, 113, 119; feedback on, 17
Wyatt, G., 53

Zull, J., 7, 82–83